Dear Reader:

The book you are about to read is the latest bestseller from the St. Martin's True Crime Library, the imprint *The New York Times* calls "the leader in true crime!" Each month, we offer you a fascinating account of the latest, most sensational crime that has captured the national attention. St. Martin's is the publisher of Tina Dirmann's VANISHED AT SEA, the story of a former child actor who posed as a yacht buyer in order to lure an older couple out to sea, then robbed them and threw them overboard to their deaths. John Glatt's riveting and horrifying SECRETS IN THE CELLAR shines a light on the man who shocked the world when it was revealed that he had kept his daughter locked in his hidden basement for 24 years. In the Edgar-nominated WRITTEN IN BLOOD, Diane Fanning looks at Michael Petersen, a Marine-turned-novelist found guilty of beating his wife to death and pushing her down the stairs of their home—only to reveal another similar death from his past. In the book you now hold, BEAUTY KILLERS, Kathy Braidhill takes a look at a dark and twisted crime spree that was anything but beautiful.

St. Martin's True Crime Library gives you the stories behind the headlines. Our authors take you right to the scene of the crime and into the minds of the most notorious murderers to show you what really makes them tick. St. Martin's True Crime Library paperbacks are better than the most terrifying thriller, because it's all true! The next time you want a crackling good read, make sure it's got the St. Martin's True Crime Library logo on the spine—you'll be up all night!

Charles E. Spicer, Jr.
Executive Editor, St. Martin's True Crime Library

TITLES BY KATHY BRAIDHILL

To Die For

Beauty Killers

**FROM THE TRUE CRIME LIBRARY
OF ST. MARTIN'S PAPERBACKS**

Beauty Killers

KATHY BRAIDHILL

St. Martin's Paperbacks

NOTE: If you purchased this book without a cover you should be aware that this book is stolen property. It was reported as "unsold and destroyed" to the publisher, and neither the author nor the publisher has received any payment for this "stripped book."

BEAUTY KILLERS

Copyright © 2010 by Kathy Braidhill.

Cover photograph by Paul Tearle, Getty Images.

All rights reserved.

For information address St. Martin's Press, 175 Fifth Avenue, New York, NY 10010.

EAN: 978-0-312-94954-9

Printed in the United States of America

St. Martin's Paperbacks edition / May 2010

St. Martin's Paperbacks are published by St. Martin's Press, 175 Fifth Avenue, New York, NY 10010.

10 9 8 7 6 5 4 3 2

This book is dedicated to Hartmut Frenzel.

Acknowledgments

I am appreciative of Hartmut Frenzel for his emotional sustenance and in awe of his tireless forays into the digital abyss to rescue the manuscript, some of which seemed more daunting than any of his six Ironmans. To my mother and sister, I give hugs and kisses for their love, patience and thoughtful care packages. And a huge hug goes to my agent, Katherine Boyle, for her understanding and tightrope navigation. Big thanks also go to Preston Li, who provided artistic relief at the barre.

Of course, this project would not be possible without the selfless dedication and persistence of the men and women in law enforcement. This case capped a long and remarkable career for DA Investigator George Hudson. George first told me about this unusual case and offered his decades of insight and invaluable experience in criminal investigation in the preparation of this work. George excels at tracking down victims who don't want to be found, which is what made a fascinating story in a prior release, "Evil Secrets," in which he located victims of violent sexual attacks that had occurred decades before. I want to extend my heartfelt appreciation to retired DA

Investigator Larry Lansford, who took over this case after George retired and saw it through to trial, penalty phase, and conviction. My thanks go to Larry for his help in getting this project off the ground.

My respect and gratitude go to Ron Garcia, now a DA investigator, his former partner, Riverside Sheriff's Department Sergeant Scott Brown, and Investigator Dave Knudson, who opened a few doors for this project.

I also to wish to thank Riverside Sheriff's Department Investigator Steve Welch, retired Investigator Allen Paine; Sargeants Richard Moker, Richard Zerkel and Patricia Knudson; retired Deputy Michael Angeli; Deputies Thomas Segobia, Roberto Albarran, and Christopher Barajas.

Many thanks go to Deputies Jacqueline Adams, Handoyo Triputra, Philip Matheny, Javier Rodriguez, Coby Webb; Sergeant Ralph Johnson; Investigators James Erickson, Carla Gordon and Robert Joseph; DA Investigators Eric Spidle, Rene Rodriguez, Ricardo Fuentes, Dave Fernandez, John Cook, Richard Houghland and Forensic Computer Technician Henry Ong, all of whom deserve recognition for their hard work.

My thanks also go to Russell Hausske, a private investigator, for his assistance with this project.

Finally, I am truly grateful for Jason Rea, who shared with me for the first time details of his startling and disturbing months of confinement with a monster, including a few things he wishes he could forget.

And most of all, I'd like to thank my readers for their support and interest in pulling back the covers on people who, for all intents and purposes could be our next-door neighbors. They fascinate and scare me as much as they do you.

Author's Note

*This is a true story,
though some names have been changed.*

One

Diane Lindholm rounded the corner in her noisy pickup truck, passing the new suburban subdivisions carved from the ranches that once dominated rural Riverside, California. One by one, ranchers had cashed out to developers, resulting in a jarring mix of empty, overgrown lots and urban sprawl next to the older mansions of monied ranchers. Lindholm, fifty, lived and worked on her own ranch, or ranchette, as purists would put it.

The two-and-a-half-acre property had a barn, two corrals where Lindholm trained horses and gave riding lessons, and a tack room to store saddles, bridles, and horse grooming gear. The ranch, where Lindholm lived with her twelve-year-old son, Eric, was two miles from a newly sprouted development of ranch-style homes whose driveways featured shiny sport utility vehicles that rarely touched dirt. Lindholm's Ford F-250 diesel truck was dusty from hauling hay and horse tack and pulling her horse trailer.

Her natural blond ringlets falling to her shoulders, Lindholm pulled into the driveway and hopped out of her truck to unlock the gate. She frowned when she saw the lock dangling from the latch and a glint from a link in the broken metal chain shining on the gravel driveway. The rest of the chain was wrapped around the gate. Lindholm's first thought was that teenagers had broken in to bother the horses, but her concern was mounting. Her son hadn't been at the bus stop waiting for her to pick him up, and it was too quiet. Where were her dogs, Zachary and Sparky?

Lindholm parked in the driveway and walked across the front lawn toward the house, not knowing whether to be annoyed or scared.

BLAM!

Lindholm froze. Gunshots were not uncommon in the semi-rural area. People sometimes shot rabbits in the seven-acre field behind her property or hunted the wild pigs that foraged in the riverbed bordering her property. Despite her fear, Lindholm was determined to check inside the house to see if her son was there. A few steps from the front door, she was startled to see someone out of the corner of her eye. A young woman with long, blond hair emerged from the breezeway adjoining the house and the tack room.

"Can I help you?" Lindholm called out to her.

"I've been hired to work here," the girl replied.

She was lying. Lindholm hadn't hired anyone. Fidgety and thin, the girl wore trendy jeans with holes at the knees and a light-colored top, hardly the type of outfit one would wear to muck out a barn or bale hay. Lindholm heard a man's voice coming from behind the vine-covered trellis that shielded the breezeway. She couldn't see the man or make out the words, but his voice was low and authoritative, as if he was giving directions. The girl looked toward the source of the voice, then back at Lindholm. She didn't know why the strange girl was on her property and began worrying about her son's whereabouts.

"O.K.," Lindholm responded, thinking quickly. "I'm just going to run inside and get a glass of water."

She tried to stay calm as she walked the remaining few yards to her front door. Once inside, she thought only of her son as she raced frantically through the house to his bedroom. She didn't notice the kitchen window pane on the counter. She tore open her son's bedroom door. He wasn't there.

She ran to the kitchen phone and dialed 9-1-1. The dispatcher told her to leave the house immediately. She was instructed to lock the house, walk slowly to her truck, drive to a neighbor's house and wait for police. As Lindholm spoke with the dispatcher, she watched the young woman standing in the breezeway, turning to her right and looking down, apparently talking with the man hiding behind the trellis. From the house, Lindholm could see only the girl. Why hadn't she moved from the breezeway?

It seemed like a very long walk back to her truck as the gravity of the moment sank in. Lindholm was too frightened to turn her head to see if the young woman was still there. She wanted to run but tried not to appear rushed or anxious. Lindholm quietly got into her truck, glancing up only to notice that the strange girl was still standing by the tack room, talking with the man hidden by the trellis.

Why would this young woman and her unseen companion break the lock to get on her property? All Lindholm had were horses, and this girl wasn't dressed like someone who knew her way around a corral. Who was behind the trellis? Did one of them fire the gun?

More importantly, where was her son?

County Gas Pumps on Etiwanda Avenue
Mira Loma, California
4:06 p.m.

"Two Edward eleven, stand by to copy. 459 in progress."

Deputy Jim Erickson turned his head slightly to talk into the compact radio microphone strapped to his chest, recognizing the penal code section for residential burglary. It was the end of the day shift and Erickson, like dozens of other deputies, was at one of the gas pumps scattered around the county topping off the tank of his cruiser.

"459 in progress," the dispatcher said. "Riverview at 46th. White female twenties, last seen wearing light-colored shirt over jeans. Possibly a male suspect, no further description. Reporting party was advised by dispatch to leave."

Erickson replaced the gas nozzle, hopped in his patrol car, and punched the accelerator. The patrol supervisor advised him to drive with lights but no siren. It would take him at least twenty minutes in the build of pre–rush hour traffic to travel the more than eight miles to the location. He took Mission Boulevard to avoid the freeway and listened to the buzz from intermittent radio calls as he drove. He recognized the voice of his supervisor, Sergeant Ralph Johnson, who said he would personally report to the Riverview address, and that of Deputy Chris Barajas, who was close to the neighborhood. Minutes later, the dispatcher broadcast reports of two intruders hopping fences in the Loring Ranch neighborhood, a fairly new residential subdivision a little over a mile from the Riverview address. Erickson heard Johnson, en route to Riverview, sending additional units to Riverview and to Loring Ranch. Dispatch was quickly flooded with calls from frightened residents in the subdivision.

Erickson was approaching the Riverview location when the radio crackled again. "Two Edward eleven, stand by to copy," the dispatcher said. "86 the response to a 459 at Riverview and 46th," the dispatcher said, giving him the code to abandon his previous assignment. Erickson listened to the new instructions: "Suspicious persons fleeing, one male, one female, no further description, southbound from location in vicinity of Loring Ranch," the dispatcher said. "Air 1 en route."

Deputy Erickson flipped on his siren, punched the brakes to spin his unit around, and sped toward Loring Ranch.

Loring Ranch
Rubidoux, California
4:15 p.m.

The twins had been squirming in the back of the van all the way home from school. Monique Bihm drove the giggling boys and their older sister through the newly built Loring Ranch subdivision. The developer had sought to carve out the maximum number of cul-de-sacs, creating a maze of look-alike, dead-end streets. Bihm swung the car right, then made a series of lefts through the labyrinth and a final left onto Ruis Court.

Loring Ranch was a project of the county redevelopment agency, whose mission was to revitalize the economically challenged part of Rubidoux. The housing tract resembled a gameboard of miniature suburbia with boxy starter homes in tiny squares of yard. Scrawny trees and ankle-high hedges afforded meager privacy, as did the proximity of homes. They were so close together, it was as easy to see into the next-door neighbor's yard as the yard several houses over. But the residents were willing to overlook such deficits in order to own a home within a two-hour freeway drive of the greater Los Angeles area.

Once Bihm turned the corner, she saw her children's chalk artwork decorating the blacktop in front of the house. She made a sharp left turn to avoid the row of chalk houses that looked just like the ones on their street, some with wisps of smoke coming out of the chimneys. She parked to the far left of the wide, concrete driveway and pushed a button on the console to unlock the passenger doors. The three kids noisily spilled out of the car and into the front yard to play. Though it was mid-April, icicle-style Christmas lights dripped from the roofline, topping the flagstone-framed picture window that overlooked the trimmed and treeless lawn.

Bihm turned around and pulled the children's backpacks from the backseat, then flipped up the visor on the driver's side for the button to the garage-door opener. Laden with book bags, Bihm walked up the driveway as the garage door yawned open to reveal a weight-lifting bench, a treadmill, and boxes of camping equipment. She walked past the garage wall of neatly hung rakes and hoes and entered the side door into the kitchen.

After piling the backpacks on the kitchen table, she made a call, cradling the phone at her shoulder while she fixed the children a snack. Then she heard the screams.

Tamara, ten, and Cameron, seven, ran past their mother into the kitchen through the side door to the garage. She rushed to the door and saw a large, brown Suburban in the garage, its front bumper rammed against the wall a few feet from the kitchen door. A middle-aged man at the wheel was gunning the engine, repeatedly slamming into the metal shelves and crushing Bihm's camping equipment as if he were trying to wedge the oversized SUV into the too-small garage. A sickening swirl of exhaust fumes quickly filled the garage as the Suburban's wheels squealed and spun on the slick concrete floor. And suddenly Bihm came face-to-face with a disturbed young woman at her kitchen door.

"Don't call the police!" cried the woman. She seemed panicked. "They're coming after us. You need to help us. Please don't call the police!"

Stunned and terrified, Bihm dropped the phone and yelled at the female intruder to get out. Instead, the thin, blonde woman pushed the kitchen door trying to force her way into the house. Fear turned to outrage as Bihm instinctively pushed back, sending the young woman sprawling. The woman quickly recovered, lunged to the left of the kitchen door and slammed her hand on the button to close the garage door. It descended, struck the Suburban's bumper, then bounced up again.

The strange but terrifying battle escalated as the young woman used all of her might to shove her way into Bihm's home while trying to close the garage door in a vain attempt to conceal the large Suburban. Bihm had to summon all of her strength to keep the woman out of her house. She occasionally locked eyes with the dark-haired man behind the wheel who fixed an angry gaze at her, as if he were indignant that she would not let them barge into her home.

Bihm frantically scanned the garage for her other son, who she thought might be cowering behind some boxes. She spotted him, stock still and panic stricken, pinned between the garage wall and the Suburban's passenger-side door that was hanging open inches from the kitchen door. It looked as though he had tried to run into the house but had become penned in when the car door swung open. The boy stood there with his arms sticking out, between the passenger-side door and the wall, just out of Bihm's reach.

Bihm screamed for him to come inside, but he stared blankly, immobilized by the noise and the confusion. She reached out of the door jamb to grab him, but the woman blocked her. Bihm yelled at the woman to get out of her garage and screamed for her son to get in the house.

"We need help," the woman yelled back, again pressing the automatic door device as the garage door banged against the Suburban. "Please don't call the police. My husband is hurt."

Bihm reflexively glanced up at the driver and, as if on cue, he dramatically slumped over toward passenger seat.

That infuriated Bihm. With a surge of adrenaline, she gave the woman a hard shove on the shoulder, sending her lurching backward. Clinging to the door frame, Bihm leaned out as far as she could, grabbed her son's shirt, and gave it a hard yank. She dragged the boy into the house, slammed the kitchen door shut, and locked it. Through the door, Bihm heard the revving car engine and the woman's screams.

With her hand in a death grip on her son's shirt, Bihm dragged him down the hall to hunt for the phone and hit the speed-dial button for 9-1-1. She released her grasp and all three children silently clung to her, too terrified to cry. Bihm and the children migrated slowly into the living room. She realized that her body ached and she was gasping for air. It had taken all of her strength to prevent the woman and her male companion from pushing into her house. As she spoke with the dispatcher, the clamor from the garage died down. Then she heard the man's voice, commanding and cold.

Bihm gave the dispatcher a description of the two intruders: The woman was thin with bleached blond hair, stood about five feet four inches tall, and wore jeans and a spaghetti-strapped shirt. Beyond that general physical description, Bihm realized that she had never seen the face of the woman with whom she had struggled, albeit on opposite sides of a kitchen door. Instead, she had locked eyes with the man behind the wheel. Bihm had been transfixed by his icy glare. She would not forget *his* face.

Bihm was still giving the 9-1-1 dispatcher information when she saw the couple on foot outside her living room window. The man sprinted out of her driveway and ran directly across the street. The woman emerged from the garage, on Bihm's right, and ran across the lawn within feet of their living room window to the next-door neighbor's house to the left.

Within moments, the man came back into view and ran in Bihm's direction calling for the woman, who did a jerky half-jog to the middle of the street to meet him. The sparse landscaping provided a full view, allowing Bihm to relay every detail of the couple's frenetic flight though the small neighborhood to the dispatcher as she watched from her living room window. The man and woman sprinted to the house across the street and seemed prepared to scale the side yard fence when a dog barked at them from the other side. The couple turned and ran across the lawn to the house next door. The man helped boost the woman over the flimsy wood stake fence into the side yard, then hoisted himself over the top and dropped out of Bihm's sight.

Aaron Rogers was working in his home office when he heard scuffling in his backyard. He didn't see anything in his own yard, but at six feet four inches, he could easily see over the fence he shared with his neighbor. Puzzled, Rogers saw a man and a woman kneeling at the water spigot by some deck chairs, rubbing their hands together under the running water. The couple's clothes were dripping wet.

"Hey, what the heck is going on?" Rogers saw his neighbor, Paul Heckel, confront the couple from his backyard patio. The couple jumped to their feet and started pacing around the tiny side yard as if deciding what to do, their movements jittery and jerky. It didn't look normal; to Rogers, it looked like they were under the influence of drugs.

Within a few minutes, Roberts heard Heckel come around to the front of the house from the street side of the gate. Heckel had a gun in his hand and he was pointing it at them.

"*Get down now*!!!" Heckel shouted. "I have a weapon and I will shoot!"

The couple ignored him and ran down the side of his house toward the back fence. Heckel had landscaped a berm, making it easier to scramble over. That fence led to the backyards of homes on Osage Avenue.

"You get on that fence and I will shoot you off the top of it. Now *get down*!!!" Heckel shouted. After a tense moment, the man's hands went to the top of the fence.

"Stop and lie facedown on the ground! Lie down on the ground now!" Heckel shouted. The couple stopped and stared. Moving in slow motion, they started to crouch down toward the ground. Then the man slowly stood and put his hands up, palms facing Heckel.

"No, no, we can't do that, sir," the man said, sounding agitated, as if he was in a hurry to get out of there. "We can't do that."

Roberts stood watching from his side of the fence and wished that the couple would just stay put. He knew Heckel didn't want to shoot unless it was absolutely necessary. The houses were so close together and the backyards were so small that less than ten feet separated him from his neighbor's side yard. Roberts stood and watched, close enough to see beads of sweat on the man's face but too far away to help. Overhead, he heard the faint but unmistakable noise of an approaching police helicopter. Roberts felt reassured that help was on the way but slightly unnerved that police had deemed it necessary to summon air support.

Heckel continued his attempts to shout the couple off the fence. The man yelled something back, but Roberts couldn't make out the words.

In a moment, the couple disappeared behind the fence and ran up the narrow side yard between the houses facing Osage Avenue.

Catrina Court had just arrived home from school when she heard a woman screaming. It sounded far away, as if someone was playing a scary movie too loud in the typically quiet neighborhood. The woman's horrified shrieks got louder, and then Catrina heard a man's voice.

Catrina, sixteen, peeked out of her bedroom window and saw the head and shoulders of a man trying to climb over the neighbor's fence. Startled, she drew back. Her bedroom window, which looked directly into the neighbor's yard, was less than twenty-five feet from where the man stood. She saw his torso pop up and down as he tried to hoist himself over the fence. After a pause, a girl emerged over the fence line as the man helped her over from the other side. With one final push, the terrified girl scrambled up and over the fence and stumbled away.

"Run, babe, run!" he shouted after her. "Keep running!"

Catrina listened to the woman's footsteps as she raced

down Crestmore Avenue, the street behind the house, and heard the effort expressed in the woman's screams as she ran. The eerie sound faded as she got further away, drowned out by the noise of an approaching police helicopter hovering over the neighborhood.

Catrina never saw the woman's face.

Lindholm Ranch
4:15 p.m.

Deputy Chris Barajas rounded the corner of Diane Lindholm's tree-studded ranch at 46th Street and Riverview and parked his marked patrol car next to two other black-and-whites outside the gate. Tall and beefy with a thatch of black hair, Barajas had been a patrol deputy at the Jurupa Valley Station in Rubidoux for nine years and knew the area well. Like the other officers based out of the Jurupa station, he was at the end of a day shift when he was dispatched to the routine burglary call. Before heading to the ranch, Barajas had picked up the house key from a tearful Lindholm, who had dutifully locked her home before escaping to a friend's house. Faced with the break-in and strangers on her property, she feared the worst regarding her son. Barajas drove back to the ranch with the key and radioed dispatch to relay the boy's description and last known whereabouts. He handed the key to the four uniformed deputies so they could walk through the house and property. The patrol officers' sole purpose was to search for intruders; under the chain of command evidence of any criminal activity had to be handled by detectives. Barajas remained outside to prevent anyone who wasn't authorized to be there from entering the property.

The deputies walked in twos, carefully stepping around the broken chain link near the gate. One pair searched the front while the other pair followed the fence line around the back. They poked through a detached toolshed and around a green vintage Volkswagen Beetle and a black horse trailer parked in the driveway. They stepped over pools of water to get to the tack room. It was messy and flooded, but they found no intruders.

Around the back of the house, the deputies found evidence of a break-in. Deep tire tracks were carved in the grass between the house and the tack room, exposing divots of soft earth. The deputies found two broken windows; near the glass shards at the rear door were a brick and a boot print.

Barajas waited at the gate for the deputies to complete their cursory search for intruders. Once they cleared the property, he radioed dispatch again so that they could notify Lindholm that she could return, and sent a deputy to pick her up. Barajas maintained control of the property until a pair of deputies arrived ten minutes later with Lindholm, tearful and upset about the encounter with the intruder and concerned about the whereabouts of her son. Barajas assured her that officers were actively looking for him.

She told Barajas about the cut lock on the gate, the gunshot, the blond intruder, and the man's voice behind the trellis. Barajas gently escorted Lindholm around the ranch to determine if anything was missing, damaged, or out of place. They started with the front gate, noting that the gravel was displaced by tire tracks, which ran from the driveway toward the back of the house. It had rained earlier in the week, making the yard soft enough for tires to turn up soil. Barajas pieced together the segments to recreate the driver's route. The tracks cut a semi-circle on the pavement between the house and the garage and around the outbuildings. From the acceleration divots in the dirt, it appeared as though the intruder had backed up the car in order to park behind the house. Lindholm had left laundry hanging out to dry on a clothesline strung from the corner of the garage to an outbuilding. The driver had mowed down the clothesline, dragging the freshly laundered clothing through the mud and leaving grassy tire impressions on a sock and a pair of underpants. Lindholm told Barajas that neither she nor her friends ever drove their cars through her backyard. When they got to the back of the house, Lindholm wept quietly when she saw the kitchen screen lying on top of the shattered glass and then more broken glass from the sliding French doors that led to the bedroom. The sliding glass door to the living room was not broken. Oddly, a coffee mug filled with pens had been removed from the kitchen, Lindholm told Barajas. She had been too consumed with the frantic search for her son when she first entered her home to notice that the mug was missing.

They followed the tread marks around the tack room and the covered stable and down to the driveway where clumps of soil clung to the cement. Dark marks in the street indicated that the driver had turned right out of the driveway and headed northbound on Riverview. Telltale rubber transfer marks in the street suggested that the driver had again stomped on the accelerator.

As they walked around the property in the fading sunlight, Lindholm pointed out several unfamiliar items: Ray-Ban sunglasses near the tree in the front yard, goldtone prescription eyeglasses a few yards away, a pink nail file near the breezeway, and a half-smoked Marlboro cigarette tossed in the dirt. They saw nothing out of the ordinary in the stable, except for Lindholm's two dogs cowering in a pile of hay. Zachary, a German shepherd, and Sparky, a medium-sized black mixed-breed, typically rushed the gate to greet visitors, Lindholm said, and rarely napped in the hay, even when it rained. Kisser, the barn cat, was nowhere to be found.

Barajas and Lindholm walked down the white latticed breezeway running alongside the tack room, which was covered by a lush, climbing vine. Someone had dragged a bright yellow hose into the tack room and turned the water on full blast. Lindholm said she always kept the hose coiled up by the faucet. Water streamed out from under the tack room door, creating a liquid crosswalk on the concrete and soaking a pair of men's plaid undershorts. Odd-looking pink clumps floated in the water. Barajas asked Lindholm if she had left the water on. She had not, nor had she noticed the water running during her encounter with the strange girl. Lindholm pointed out that the missing mug of pens from the kitchen was sitting on an upturned pail just beyond the breezeway. As they moved closer to the tack room, they both noticed droplets of blood just outside the entrance.

The door to the tack room was open. Lindholm said that she always kept the door locked with a padlock slipped through an eyelet-type latch, but the padlock was missing. Barajas poked his head in the room, but one of the windows had been draped with a horse blanket, dimming the meager sunlight. When his eyes adjusted, he stopped in his tracks.

Barajas saw blood—a lot of it. Blood and bits of flesh splattered one wall. The other end of the yellow hose had flooded the room, diluting a mass of blood that had pooled on the floor and soaking a soft-sided yellow and green rifle case next to an upturned bucket to the right of the door. Fistfuls of duct tape tangled with strands of hair, follicles intact, lay wadded on the floor. Lindholm peered over Barajas's shoulder and gasped. Barajas leaned over and turned off the hose to prevent the destruction of critical evidence. There was too much blood for anything less than a life-threatening injury and since the deputies' search hadn't turned up anyone on the property, they needed to find the injured person—whether he or she was a perpetrator or a victim.

Barajas quietly backed Lindholm out of the tack room and explained that she should stay with friends or family for the night while the detectives and criminalists processed her property for evidence. He needed to radio dispatch and seal off the property, which was now a crime scene. The amount of blood indicated this was not just a simple burglary. He made a mental note to phone his wife: it was going to be a very long night.

Barajas walked Lindholm down the driveway, pausing periodically to number, fold, and place three-by-five-inch index cards next to potential evidence. He placed the small cards next to the sunglasses, the nail file, a park schedule, and, by the gate, a grim bit of metal illuminated by the final rays of sunset—a .38-caliber live round.

**Loring Ranch
4:28 p.m.**

As Deputy Erickson entered the twisted maze of streets that comprised the Loring Ranch development, he heard from Sergeant Johnson, who hadn't made it over to the Lindholm ranch either. Johnson was a few minutes ahead of him and the other units were en route. Air 1, the police helicopter, had the fleeing suspects in sight and was broadcasting their location. The pilot's bird's-eye view, however, made it impossible to see street addresses, so he described the direction, the street, and identifying landmarks like trees, fences, and house colors. The suspects had abandoned their car on Ruiz Court, the pilot told them, and were fleeing on foot. As they scaled fences and fled through backyards, the pilot helped Erickson, Johnson, and a growing trail of black-and-whites navigate the confusing cul-de-sacs.

"All units. Suspects on foot, southbound from Ruiz Court to Osage," the helicopter pilot said. Erickson was one street over. As he turned down Westerfield Street, he heard the pilot say that the suspects were five houses from the corner of Westerfield and Osage. Then Sergeant Johnson said that he had the male suspect in sight.

Erickson drove three blocks down Westerfield, and as soon as he turned left on Osage, he could see Johnson's black-and-white parked at the fifth house from the corner. Erickson pulled up, leaped out of his car, and ran toward the yard where he saw Johnson near the picket fence, pointing his service revolver at a man standing inches away on the other side. The man stood calmly with his hands raised.

Johnson shouted over the deafening *chop-chop-chop* of the helicopter as Erickson approached without taking his eyes off the suspect: "He's back here! He's back here!" Johnson directed Erickson to a gate on the west side of the house.

Erickson sprinted around the side to the backyard gate. It was locked. The burly officer stepped back and kicked it open, pulling his service revolver from his holster while doubling back to the side yard so he was on the same side of the fence as the detained suspect. Once Erickson came within view, Johnson lowered his weapon.

The man, clad in blue jeans, a dark T-shirt, and odd-looking rubber shoes, offered no resistance. Erickson holstered his weapon and reached for his handcuffs; he noted that the suspect was dripping wet, from head-to-toe.

"Am I in trouble? I just went back there to wash off because I was hot," the man said.

"What's your name?" Erickson asked, as he cuffed him quietly. He noticed scrapes and some blood on the man's hands.

"Mike," the man answered. The helicopter buzzed away, and they could finally speak without shouting.

"Mike, what's your last name?" Erickson asked, leading him back around the house and toward the street. "Mike" didn't respond. Erickson tried again: "Mike, do you live around here?" No answer. Erickson knew that suspects sometimes ignored questions from police, so he did not ask again. The man offered no resistance and was otherwise cooperative. Erickson directed him to the front of the patrol car, patted him down for weapons, and emptied his pockets. Erickson pulled out his wallet, a wad of cash, which was also soaking wet, and a padlock that had been painted black. He placed the bills on the windshield, using the wiper blade to prevent them from being blown away, as was standard practice. He put the wallet and padlock next to it. The suspect had nothing else in his pockets.

Johnson directed Erickson to put the suspect in the backseat of Deputy Michelle Couchman's unit.

By this time, a mass of patrol cars had converged on the small cul-de-sac. Sergeant Johnson's responsibility as the on-scene patrol supervisor was to coordinate with the watch captain, the supervisor of detectives, and the county crime lab and to manage the response of deputies to the different crime scenes. With one ear tuned to radio traffic, he learned that the search at the Lindholm ranch had turned up no intruders, but Barajas had found a large quantity of blood in the tack room. Johnson had deployed a contingent of deputies to Loring Ranch and had split assignments for the incoming evening shift of deputies between the two crime scenes. Johnson was relieved to hear that Lindholm's son had been found unharmed at a friend's house and reunited with his mother, which allowed detectives to rule out the boy as a victim. But the fleeing female seemed to have vanished into thin air.

The homeowners who had watched the drama from behind closed doors gathered in clusters on their front lawns, gawking at the handcuffed man who had been running through their backyards just minutes before. Johnson asked Deputy Couchman and her partner to arrange an in-field identification of the suspect by the residents who had reported seeing the intruders. But before she could begin that process, some of the residents approached Johnson.

Paul Heckel, who had chased away the trespassers with his wife's service revolver, spoke to Johnson first. Right behind him was his neighbor and the family that lived across the street. Johnson told all of them that a deputy would bring the suspect to them for identification within the hour. But Heckel shook his head. He had something to show to Johnson.

"They buried something in my yard," Heckel said, pointing to his house across the street from where "Mike" had been cornered and arrested. Johnson followed Heckel through his backyard, which much like his own backyard,

was half grass and half dirt. Heckel walked around to
the side yard and pointed out odd lumps sticking out of
loose soil in a planter next to the gas meter. On the other
side of the fence, Johnson found more of the suspects'
half-buried belongings.

Criminals fleeing on foot typically make frenzied attempts to rid themselves of loot, weapons, or drugs. These
suspects had inexplicably dropped an array of debris that
bore more of a resemblance to an upturned kitchen junk
drawer than smoking-gun evidence of a crime: hearts-
and-flowers design postage stamps; a six-milliliter bottle
of Clear Eyes solution; an owner's manual for a Radio
Shack DR-E11 160-minute digital recorder; a package of
Starburst candy; a receipt for a local auto parts store; a
pair of green dice with white dots; a lottery ticket; business cards for a sign and banner store and a janitorial service; two butane lighters, one red and one black with
"Chris" and the other with "Mike" hand-scratched on the
side; a yellow metal key chain with fifteen keys and a foam
toy; a flowered, yellow metal pill box containing three
pills; a clear glass vial containing multicolored rocks; a
camouflage eyeglass retaining cord; a silver-colored folding knife on a belt clip; a black Nokia flip-style cell
phone; a plastic container; six checks to a hair salon; a
white metal key chain with a silver metal screw-top container; and a silver necklace and earrings.

Johnson radioed dispatch for a forensic technician to
bag and tag the items. Although Erickson had checked
the suspect in custody for blood, Johnson wanted to take
a closer look at him to see if he bore any injuries consistent
with the amount of blood found at the ranch. He walked
over to Deputy Couchman's patrol car where "Mike" sat
handcuffed in the backseat and shined a flashlight on the
suspect's face and neck area. The suspect was dripping
wet, but Johnson didn't see any blood or injuries. When
the forensic technician arrived, she would photograph
his hands and upper torso, inspect him for cuts or other
injuries, and swab for gunshot residue. Additional photos

would be taken when he was booked at the jail. Johnson directed a deputy to take the detained suspect from the backseat and allow each neighbor, in turn, a look at the man to see if they could identify him as the person who had run through their yards. As the deputy helped him out of the patrol car, the man started asking questions.

"Where is my friend?" the man asked.

"What are you talking about?" the deputy replied, hoping to prompt an answer from the suspect about the second fleeing intruder.

"Crystal," the man said. "She has blond hair. I helped her over the back wall so she could get away."

The deputy asked the suspect to stand by a wall so that a forensic tech could take photos of his hands. He complied, but asked again and again about the girl.

"Where's Crystal?" he asked. "Where's Crystal?"

Crestmore Avenue
Rubidoux, California
4:45 p.m.

The hysterical young woman sprang out in front of Richard Horgan's county-issued truck. Horgan peered out from behind the steering wheel and slowed to a stop to avoid hitting her. A maintenance carpenter for the county parks system, Horgan was returning to the facility at Rancho Jurupa Park after working all day in Idyllwild, about sixty miles away. He was headed back to county park headquarters on Crestmore Avenue when the woman ran up to his truck, yanked open the passenger-side door, and jumped in.

"Get me out of here!" she cried.

The mild-mannered carpenter tried telling the young woman that he wasn't allowed to give people rides in county vehicles, but she drowned him out.

"Four guys are chasing me!" she said. "They're trying to kill me! Go, go, go!"

Horgan looked at the petite woman occupying his passenger seat. Straight blond hair, tiny jeans, a light-colored tank top. She was breathing heavily, her tank top was dripping wet, and she looked petrified.

Horgan hit the gas.

Lindholm Ranch
Rubidoux, California
April 17, 2001, 6 p.m.

"Someone died in here," said Detective Scott Brown. He was standing at the door of the tack room looking at the blood. At his shoulder was his partner, Detective Ron Garcia. Brown and Garcia had been the on-call detectives that night for the Jurupa Valley Station. The seasoned detectives each had been driving home after working the day shift when they were summoned back to work at 5:30 p.m. to investigate the report of intruders and possibly blood at 46th and Riverview. Nearing forty, Brown was tall and sported a thatch of salt-and-pepper hair. Like Garcia, he was still clad in the clothes he had worn to work that day.

Garcia nodded his head. He was stout, with a clean-shaven head and known for his well-cut suits. Both detectives had noted the light pinkish clots of arterial blood still lingered in the walkway despite the perpetrators' attempt to wash them down. Few people recover from such a profound loss of blood.

If Brown and Garcia had been assigned this case just one month before, they would have taken control of the crime scene immediately and plunged into their work. But on this night, they were forced to do the most difficult thing one can do at a fresh crime scene: wait. Garcia got on the phone and called the Central Homicide Unit, CHU. Based in downtown Riverside, CHU was comprised of detectives who handle cases countywide. It replaced the former system in which each of the eleven sheriff's stations in the greater Riverside County area investigated its own homicides. It seemed to Garcia as if an eternity had passed before a supervisor from CHU finally called back with a critical question: Where's the body? Absent a body that represented tangible evidence of a homicide, CHU wouldn't roll out. Frustrated, Garcia and Brown were shoehorned into bureaucratic vapor lock. The two detectives, each on their cell phones at the crime scene, marched up and down the sheriff's department chain of command for hours, stalled by the new unit's lack of protocol for a situation in which there was no corpse to show that a homicide indeed had occurred. The detectives had asked dispatch to alert local and regional hospitals and urgent care clinics to report any gunshot victim who had sustained substantial blood loss, but so far no one had turned up. Garcia and Brown parked deputies at the crime scenes, and the criminalists sat on their hands, unable to process the scenes for evidence until CHU delivered its final answer. While they waited, the first few precious hours, deemed the most critical immediately following a homicide, slipped away. The rapid-fire succession of events had caught the large station between shifts, as deputies and detectives scrambled to respond to three crime scenes within a mile or two of one another. At one point in the early evening, there were scant deputies available to respond to other calls, much less provide routine traffic patrol.

By 10 p.m., supervisors delivered a decision to Garcia and Brown: CHU would not respond without a body, meaning that the detectives had the authority to proceed with the investigation. With their role finally clarified, Garcia and Brown would be the primary detectives, responsible for overseeing the investigation, conducting major interviews, writing out reports and search warrants, telling the uniforms what to do, and acting as liaisons with higher-ups in the department. The secondary detectives would process the crime scenes and feed the primaries information. Once the detectives received the go-ahead, they wasted no time pulling Detectives Dave Knudson and Steve Welch out of bed to process the garage and the ranch. Knudson was assigned to process the Lindholm ranch and Welch was sent to Monique Bihm's garage. When Welch finished, he would shadow Knudson as he processed the homicide scene. Welch had recently been promoted from deputy to detective and had just finished detective training. First, he had been shipped off to an outlying station to be a one-man detective unit for a few weeks, handling everything but homicide and sexual assault cases; then he began to take on sexual assault cases and finally spent another year shadowing senior detectives on homicides. Primed and ready to begin handling homicides, the lucky detective would finally work his first homicide on his own.

Loring Ranch
April 17, 2001

The excitement of the chase had died down in the Loring Ranch neighborhood long before Welch arrived. At this late hour, the modest residential neighborhood had been overtaken by jumpsuited forensic technicians, who labored behind the yellow crime scene tape that outlined the intruders' flight path. Like a reality police show unfolding before their eyes, neighbors had been treated to an exciting chase and the arrest of a suspect followed by a perp stroll in which they were allowed to view the man, flanked by deputies, and signal whether he looked like the same individual who had run through their yards. The middle-aged male suspect was wearing flat, odd-looking loafers made of neoprene, the waterproof material used to make wetsuits. Still damp, he was driven around the small cul-de-sacs to informal, in-field lineups, waving and identifying himself to residents as if he were campaigning for office.

The distraught female suspect who had hailed the truck was driven by the parks worker straight to his headquarters a mile down the road. The woman told a wild story, claiming she was chased by four men who wanted to kill her and her friend "Tracy," and was desperate to phone police. Once the woman was inside, an office worker dialed 9-1-1, only she apparently experienced a change of heart and instead wanted to call a friend. She ran to a desk and upended the contents of her purse to search, she said, for a phone number, then panicked and crawled under a desk. By the time police arrived, she was curled up in the fetal position under the desk, shivering and wet. The officer, who at this time suspected that she was the second fleeing suspect, coaxed the soaked and distraught woman out from under the desk and escorted her back to the neighborhood from which she had just escaped. After separate lineups with each suspect, the neighbors who had poured into the street to watch the drama finally succumbed and returned to their homes, leaving the technicians to take measurements and photos and collect evidence in silence.

Back in Monique Bihm's garage, Welch crouched and cocked an eyebrow at the odd potpourri spilling out of the brown Suburban through the open driver's side door: a dark green pillowcase, a zipper-lock plastic bag, a dirty, one-by-one foot sheet of glass, and a recently oiled hunting knife. What, Welch wondered, was this couple running from? Why were they trying to hide? A twelve-year veteran of the Riverside County Sheriff's Department, he had never seen anyone try to hide their truck in someone else's garage. At first glance, the light brown Suburban appeared well lived in. To Welch, it resembled a pack rat's nest, with clothing, shoes, paperwork, and tools stuffed into every corner. In the driver's haste to exit the car, he had inadvertently kicked some of his belongings onto the garage floor. Welch found two interesting tidbits on the windshield. Taped to the inside of the windshield

on the driver's side was a receipt for nearby Rancho Jurupa Park, and under the wiper blade he found a piece of
cardboard with "Vinnie! 6014" written on it, perhaps indicating the number of the campsite. A camping trip
could explain the mess inside the truck. Jurupa Park was
a mile or two away and could yield more clues. He asked
the forensic tech to bag the items.

Except for the large, light brown Suburban sticking
out of it, the garage was otherwise well-organized. Rakes,
brooms, and gardening equipment were neatly hung against
one wall, a weight set and bench were on the opposite
side, and children's bicycles and a plastic child-size basketball stand and hoop occupied the spot for the second
car in the two-car garage. Welch walked around the Suburban and looked through the windows. The front windows were down, but the back windows were tinted and
rolled up. Welch spotted a black folding wallet on the
bench seat behind the driver's side and asked the latex-
gloved technician to photograph it. After snapping the
shot, the forensic tech reached in and pulled the wallet
off the seat.

The wallet contained various forms of photo identification bearing the name Janeen Marie Snyder. Welch did
not know whether the ID belonged to the woman who
was arrested at Rancho Jurupa Park or to the presumed
victim. Maybe it belonged to someone who the couple
had robbed. There was a Social Security card, a World
Savings Bank ATM card, and a nongaming card, a required credential for employees of businesses that allow
gambling. It took Welch about forty-five minutes to look
through the garage for evidence, and then he left the forensic tech to photograph and collect the items. Before he
left Loring Ranch for the Riverview location, he spoke
with Sergeant Johnson, the patrol supervisor, who told
Welch that he would arrange to have the vehicle towed to
the crime lab's garage for processing. Then he checked in
with Garcia and Brown to tell them that he was finished
and was going to head over to the Lindholm property.

Even though more clues lay hidden in the Suburban, Welch could not give it a more thorough search without a warrant.

Lindholm Ranch
Rubidoux, California
11:40 p.m.

The headlights of Sergeant Dave Knudson's county-issued blue Taurus illuminated a light mist settling on the swarm of patrol cars outside the gate of the Lindholm ranch. With barns, corrals, and grazing pasture outnumbering homes in the neighborhood, the unmistakable aroma of horses filled the air. Tall, burly and balding, Knudson had been ready to crawl into bed after working patrol all day. When the phone rang at 10:30 p.m., he'd been looking forward to a good night's sleep. Knudson had been aware of the chase after the intruders at Riverview fled to Loring Ranch, but he was off-duty when the grisly details of the Lindholm ranch scene had finally hit the police airwaves.

"Hey, Dave," Detective Garcia had told a sleepy Knudson. "The barn is full of blood. There's so much blood that it's seeping under the tack room door."

Garcia added that they had seen clumps of light pink arterial blood floating in the walkway. He described the concentration of blood they saw in one area of the tack room and the lack of a blood trail. The quantity of blood and the presence of arterial clots indicated to the experienced detectives that there was a dead body somewhere; the absence of a blood trail told them that the person had died right there, unless the attempt to hose down the tack room had also washed away the blood trail. So which was it? Either the intruders had hidden the body somewhere on the property, or the victim survived, at least long enough to leave the grounds. Since they couldn't immediately locate a body, it was a mystery to them how anyone could survive such an enormous blood loss. If the victim was still alive, why was there no blood trail?

Knudson was not happy about being called out late at night, not only because he was tired, but because he was not particularly fond of the mundane task of processing a crime scene. He liked tracking people—witnesses, victims and suspects—and getting them to talk. Holding the other end of a measuring tape was not much fun, but he didn't have a choice. Nonetheless, Knudson dressed quickly and headed out the front door to the Lindholm ranch.

After soaring into the mid-eighties earlier in the day, the temperature was quickly dropping into the thirties. Detectives in suits and deputies in uniforms stamped their feet and clutched styrofoam coffee cups, their breath coming in puffs as they waited outside the gate to the ranch. Yellow crime-scene tape swathed its circumference, stretching from the chain-link fence at the front of the property to the small stream that formed the boundary at the rear. By the time Knudson rolled up the front gate a half-hour after Garcia's call, he found Deputy Barajas still on duty. He told Knudson that one of the county's dog handlers would arrive soon with a bloodhound and no one was allowed on the property, so Knudson returned to his car to wait. They couldn't contaminate the scene with additional human scents until the dog had the chance to suss out a third person. It was a new experience for Knudson to wait for a dog and handler, but this particular K-9 team had worked on some notable cases, including a high-profile, successful capture of an escaped convict in San Bernardino, the neighboring county.

Knudson climbed into the Taurus and turned on the heater while he waited. Garcia's earlier description of the gory crime scene played in his head while he peered into the cold, dark night. He couldn't help feeling like he was in the middle of a horror story, a sitting duck waiting outside a bloody crime scene. He wasn't scared, but it felt a little creepy. Knudson thought he could use this down-time to call his wife.

Sergeant Patti Knudson, a nineteen-year veteran of the Riverside County Sheriff's Department, was working the graveyard shift at the jail and had her ear tuned to radio chatter when Dave called. He told Patti what he knew about both crime scenes and the capture of two suspects, one male and one female. They still didn't have a handle on the status of the third person, or whether it was a victim or another suspect and if they were severely injured or deceased. Patti said she would keep an eye out for the incoming female suspect and would process the inmate herself. Then Dave saw something move out of the corner of his eye. He said good-bye to his wife and got out of the Taurus.

"Hi Jackie," Knudson called out. Forensic technician Jacqueline Clark had spent the late afternoon and evening with Garcia and Brown, who had split their time between the Lindholm Ranch and the Loring Ranch subdivision. Her first task had been to take a series of photographs documenting the condition of the male suspect, with particular focus on his hands, arms and upper body, to determine whether he was the source of the blood in the tack room. She saw scratches on his right palm, possibly from climbing fences, but no injuries severe enough to account for the blood in the tack room. She also swabbed his hands for gunshot residue. But the most arduous task so far had been to mark, collect, and photograph the items the fleeing suspects had buried in the neighbors' backyards as well as the odd assortment of belongings that had cascaded from the brown Suburban in Monique Bihm's garage.

As Barajas was about to brief Jackie, Welch arrived, as did Garcia and Brown, and Sergeant Richard Mokar, the head of detectives at the Jurupa Valley station. They chatted for a while until Coby Webb arrived with the dog. Deputy Barajas filled them in about the crime scene and the evidence he had spotted and marked. The first wave of processing involved the dog, so only a small group would go in: Barajas, Webb with the dog, Knudson,

Welch, and Clark By the time they got on the property, it was already after midnight.

The dog's job was to look for a person. Webb's job was to look after the dog. Knudson and Barajas would keep an eye out for anything unexpected and protect the handler, if need be, while the dog did its job. Welch, still considered the new guy, was there to watch and learn. Inside the front gate, they followed the dog in single file as it trotted straight up the driveway and made a beeline for the tack room. But Detectives Garcia and Brown had said that they didn't want the dog in the tack room where it could disturb evidence. Webb called the dog back and reiterated the command, but again the dog headed straight for the tack room. Webb gave the dog a command to search the rest of the property, taking time to daub gauze rounds, called scent pads, on various items that the dog sniffed. She handed the pads to Clark to book into evidence. The dog handler directed the dog to every corner of the ranch that could possibly conceal an injured or dead person, but the dog found no one, dead or alive. However, Webb told Knudson that the dog's sense of smell was distorted by the prevalence of urine from the Lindholms' cats, which contained ammonia.

After hours of waiting for the department brass to arm-wrestle CHU over which agency would handle the case, then a bit more time waiting for the dog to arrive and search the property, the detectives were finally able to get down to the business of processing the crime scene. They congregated in the driveway and lined up single file for the walk-through. Barajas took the lead, followed by primary detectives Garcia and Brown, Knudson, Clark, and Sergeant Mokar. Welch brought up the rear. Barajas led them through the house, the barn, and the corrals like a slow-moving, segmented train, each of them carefully stepping in Barajas's footsteps to avoid contaminating the scene. Their powerful, department-issue flashlights illuminated their first in-depth look at the evidence in ghostly pockets of shadow and light. Barajas pointed out the few items he had marked: the broken gate padlock, the bullet in the driveway, the misplaced coffee cup in the breezeway, the glasses in the front yard. They saw dog food and water bowls, but the dogs were somewhere else on the property. He pointed out the tire tracks in the dirt and tread marks on the pavement, which seemed to indicate that the driver had backed the car into the backyard and parked it behind the house where Lindholm could not have seen it, either from the driveway or from where she had been standing in her front yard. Without a forensic examination of the track marks, it was not possible to determine whether more than one vehicle had been driven on the property.

Barajas guided the detectives through the house, noting the displaced screen from the kitchen window lying on the kitchen counter, which had been pushed in from the outside. The apparent point of entry was at the back of the house, where there was damage to two sliding windows. One had contact damage, suggesting someone had thrown something against the glass and left a mark. The other one had a bootprint. Jacqueline Clark would later lift the bootprint as one would a fingerprint. While it was clear that intruders had broken in, the house didn't look right to the detectives. Typical burglars tear up a house looking for jewelry, electronics, cash, or other valuables. Thieves leave hanging wires and a dust void where a TV, computer, or stereo would sit, and closet doors stand open, belongings are pulled out of drawers, and the contents of jewelry boxes dumped. Diane Lindholm's house was tidy and undisturbed. The troubling implication was that stealing property and valuables was not on the minds of these burglars.

As they walked through the house, Knudson and Clark placed numbered and folded index cards to mark each item of evidence. Each area was photographed before and after they placed the evidence markers. Clark looked for fingerprints, palm prints, and shoe impressions on the frames, trim, and glass of the sliding glass door in the living room and the kitchen window. She took photographs of the broken glass in the bedroom, and the window screen that had been removed in the kitchen, obvious signs of forced entry. She would wait until after the walk-through to complete the documentation of the crime scene and the evidence. She would take additional photos, lift as many prints as possible in the field, and then take measurements, with Knudson's help, of each outbuilding, paying particular attention to the tack room. Clark and Knudson would take turns bagging and tagging each item of evidence.

Once Clark and the detectives finished reviewing the evidence in the house, they circled through the front yard, noting the cut padlock and live round from the driveway, gold metal prescription eyeglasses, and a blue vinyl address book and calendar. They peered into a horse trailer and the vintage Volkswagen on a blacktop pad that connected the driveway to the tack room and the storage shed, but found nothing to collect. They worked their way around the back, then came through the corral, where they saw a torn half of a green, spaghetti-strap woman's shirt. It was slightly damp and lying atop hay near the corral next to the tack room. They did not see the other half of the shirt. It wasn't clear whether it was a laundry item that had been ripped from the clothesline when the intruders tore into the yard or an item of clothing left by the intruders. More intriguing items of evidence were found in the latticed, vine-covered breezeway outside the tack room where Diane Lindholm said she had seen the young woman and heard the man's voice. Clark found a shoe impression in the dirt on the other side of the the breezeway. Barajas had already placed a numbered card next to the mug containing markers and pens that had been removed from the kitchen and placed on an upturned bucket. They also found a burnt butt from a Marlboro cigarette. But something was missing. Both Knudson and Barajas had seen a pair of men's undershorts on the breezeway outside the tack room door. As with the torn green shirt, they didn't know whether it was related to this scene or whether the shorts had been dislodged from the clothesline, but now they were gone. Like the old-fashioned game of Telephone, word quickly passed down the line to Garcia, Brown, Sergeant Mokar, and finally to Welch. The property had been sealed off since shortly after 4 p.m. when the first deputies arrived at the scene. The detectives had no explanation for the missing evidence. Was there a third intruder still on the property? Was someone watching them? Though all of the detectives were armed with service revolvers, Knudson felt uneasy and Welch looked over his shoulder.

Just past dawn, after hours of circling what was considered the staging area of the crime, the detectives and Clark arrived at the door of the tack room, an unadorned twenty-by-twenty-foot room with a cement floor and exposed wood walls. The tack room housed horse equipment like saddles, lead ropes, leather crops, bridles, blankets and grooming tools, and several boxes of personal items. On Saturday, three days before, Lindholm had cleaned and hosed out the room, stacking boxes, tools, and toys on storage shelves, perching saddles on racks and neatly hanging halters and leads on hooks, leaving nothing cluttering the floor. The detectives paused at the entrance to the room to look at what the intruders had been after.

It looked to the detectives like a slaughterhouse gone awry. They saw blood everywhere, in every direction, as if someone had ritualistically splattered it from one end of the room to the other. Now dried and turning rust-brown, the blood stretched high on the walls, seeped into a poster, spattered a blanket, a shovel, backpacks, and horse equipment. Blood had saturated wood studs and clung to exposed insulation. An antique anvil that was a gift from Lindholm's uncle was upside down and sprayed with blood.

Hours after Barajas had turned off the hose, a few puddles among ominous, dark spots on the floor and a towel sopping up water in the corner behind the door were all

that remained of the suspects' attempt to clean up. As if
to discourage prying eyes, the intruders had draped a
horse blanket over the window facing the street. Wads of
gray duct tape tangled with long strands of hair and bundles of bloodied plastic cable ties littered the floor. The
long nose of a rifle poked out among the horse equipment
and storage boxes that had been pulled down from the
shelves, and next to an overturned fan by the east wall lay
one shiny shell casing.

Robert Presley Detention Center
Riverside, California
April 18, 2001, 12:12 a.m.

"Stand still," Deputy Alberto Albarran said. "Look up at
the camera."
    The fidgety young woman in the bright orange jail
jumpsuit tilted her head and glared at the camera from
under her bleached blond hair. Albarran snapped the
booking photo of the female suspect and handed custody
of the new inmate to a female deputy for processing. Albarran had driven both suspects, male and female, from
the Rancho Jurupa County Jail to the Robert Presley Detention Center, the county's primary jail facility in downtown Riverside. Albarran had taken custody of the blood
drawn from both suspects and booked it, along with the
man's belongings. He was identified as Michael Thornton, forty-two, and he had been wearing dark blue jeans,
a black T-shirt, and blue nylon aqua shoes, designed by
Nike for pool workouts. Thornton had been saturated
with water at the time of his arrest, and his clothing was
still damp. Albarran booked the clothing and placed it in
the jail's drying room for wet evidence. He separately
booked the personal effects of the suspect that had no
evidentiary value: his wallet, a Motel 6 room key, and a
bank deposit stub. He also had some cash and a black padlock. Albarran separately booked the female detainee's

clothing: light-colored blue jeans ripped at the knees with a small butterfly patch on the front, a strappy Calvin Klein top, and black lace-up boots. She had a handbag, which he gave to the female deputy to be processed in the women's wing of the jail.

The female detainee was escorted by the female deputy, shuffling in soft-soled prison-issue loafers designed to deter any inmate who might contemplate sprinting, though they wouldn't get far in the locked facility. The deputy handed the inmate and her purse to Sergeant Patricia Knudson, who had been alerted by her husband and had been awaiting the arrival of this inmate. Knudson reached inside her pocket and flipped on a concealed microcassette recorder.

"Have a seat over there," Knudson said to the inmate, motioning toward a bench. She complied. Knudson needed to search the inmate's purse and retrieve items of evidentiary value, then assess her medical and psychological condition, sexual orientation, and gang affiliation for the purpose of assigning her a housing unit. She would also take her fingerprints and run them through the state and federal computer to see if anything popped up.

Knudson reviewed the routine information Albarran already had taken to book the inmate, recording her date of birth and social security number. Janeen Snyder was twenty-one, five feet four inches, and 105 pounds. Knudson examined the purse and noted there was no wallet. She found a bank deposit slip with the name of a hair salon and a Verizon calling card. Knudson asked Snyder a few questions, but she seemed distracted. Knudson saw a very small plastic container, about the size of a marble, with a sheen of white residue. If it was methamphetamine or cocaine, it would explain Snyder's distracted condition, but there wasn't enough to test so she didn't retain it as evidence. Then she recited to Snyder the charges for which she was being booked. Knudson had been aware of the issue involving CHU during the course of the evening and knew that the detectives were desperately searching for a body or an injured person. That also posed a legal wrinkle when it came to holding the male and female suspects in custody. Without a victim, or a body, the suspects could only be booked for trespass and residential burglary, despite the blood drenching the tack room.

Knudson reached into Snyder's purse again and felt her skin crawl when she pulled out a photo ID card. Issued by the Clark County Health District in Las Vegas, the card depicted a clear color photo of a pretty, smiling teenager named Michelle Leann Curran.

TWO

**Sonic burger drive-in
Las Vegas, Nevada
April 3, 2001, 7 p.m.**

"Fine guy in Lane 4!"

The petite, dark-haired girl on roller blades whirled around her best friend, Kasey Raub, en route to the next customer. In her first night at her new job as a Sonic car hop, Michelle Curran had wasted no time scoping out cute guys. A typical sixteen-year-old, she liked "sk8er bois" who, in the pop culture patois of singer Avril Lavigne, were skinny, spiky-haired guys in baggy pants who rode skateboards.

"Go check him out," a grinning Michelle told Kasey as she wheeled away.

Best friends Michelle, Kasey and Denise Vela had applied together for jobs at Sonic, were hired together, and trained together. Michelle liked working with her friends. In their first jobs as Santa's helpers, the girls had entertained children and parents while they waited in line for Santa, then got the younger ones to smile for the camera.

The girls liked showing up to a mall for work, and were Santa's helpers the next year, too. At the center of Michelle's circle of friends was her older sister, Tiffani. Barely one year apart, the sisters formed the hub of a tight-knit, popular clique that thrived on constant contact. When they weren't together, they all stayed in touch by phone.

The petite sisters not only shared friends, they shared clothes, a basement bedroom, and a bed, since the small room wouldn't accommodate two beds. The teenagers predictably fought over the bathroom and sharing clothes. Expensive designer jeans were the subject of heated negotiations to ensure that neither of them would be seen wearing the same jeans on successive days. Michelle and Tiffani wore an enviably small size, 1, and they were proud of it. Looking good was of critical importance for both girls and a way of life for Michelle. She preferred street style over high fashion: Etnies shoes, Bongo jeans, specialty T-shirts. She dispensed style tips to her inner circle, giving one friend's casino T-shirt a thumbs-down and advising another not to wear white shirts to school.

School was also important to Michelle, not so much for the academics, but because the classroom was the perfect venue for socializing. Though she didn't care for Shakespeare or the Pythagorean theorem, she was an expert in Revlon, Max Factor, and Maybelline and diligently did her homework each night. The budding beautician practiced doing her makeup and hair as a test run for school the next day. If something didn't turn out right, she started over. Michelle laid out two different outfits each night so that she would have a choice of what to wear the next morning. She had always struggled with her studies and had been held back a grade in elementary school. At sixteen, she was a sophomore at Western High School where Tiffani was a senior. Both girls occasionally skipped classes, sometimes with their grandmother's permission. According to school policy, students who missed ten classes would fail their grade, so Michelle and Tiffani carefully planned and counted their ditch days. So far,

Tiffani had just four ditch days, but Michelle had a few more than that.

The girls lived with their grandmother, Jacqueline Deliz, in the not-so-glamorous suburbs of Las Vegas, where the median strips were landscaped with a desert palette of red-pink rocks and cactus. Nestled in a cluster of cul-de-sacs a few streets away from Highway 95, the yellow house with a palm tree in the front yard had been purchased by their uncle Bill from their grandmother. He lived there with Deliz and the two girls. The girls' mother, Candi, also lived with Deliz but alternated between staying there and with her boyfriend closer to downtown. Their aunt Kai lived a few blocks away, practically across the street from their high school, and they frequently stopped there on the way to and from school. Their grandmother didn't understand why the girls didn't just ride their bicycles to school, but Michelle and Tiffani had deemed bikes uncool. The girls either got a ride from their mother or walked. Deliz worked as a housekeeper at a casino on the Strip, a quick fifteen minutes from home.

Growing up in the shadow of Sin City held little influence over Michelle and Tiffani's posse, other than an occasional group foray to celebrate their friendship by playfully mocking suburbanites and foreign visitors. The tourists who flocked to the famed Las Vegas Strip unwittingly provided entertainment for the girls, steady employment for their families, and fueled the city's residential sprawl. Single-family homes, apartments, and ubiquitous strip malls unfurled in all directions from the city's center, making the greater Las Vegas area one of the largest and fastest-growing bedroom communities in the country. Suburbanites at heart, the girls were mainly interested in hair, makeup, clothes, and boys, boys, boys. Like any typical teenager, Michelle bounced from guy to guy. Until she met Steve.

In mid-February, Michelle had flagged down a car full of guys cruising Western High School and sauntered over to them in full flirt mode, even though her confidence belied a deep insecurity. Born with a cleft palate, Michelle bore a slight dimple on her upper lip as a result of the surgery she had had as a toddler to repair it. Among the boys sitting in the car was Steven Mahoney, a seventeen-year-old at Cimarron High School across town. Michelle was intrigued by him, and he took an interest in her as well. After a few dates and many hours on the phone, casual interest flowered into full-fledged infatuation.

Whether it was simple teenage obsession or the convenience of mobile phones, Steve and Michelle never went more than four or five hours without some form of contact and would talk on the phone for up to three hours at a time. When they were in school or when Michelle was at work, they'd write each other letters. The young couple stayed on the phone every night until bedtime. Steve was waiting for Michelle when she finished her Sonic shift that night. Though he didn't have a license, his mother drove him to the burger joint so that he could spend a few minutes with her, give her the letter he wrote while she was at work, and escort her home. That night, like every night, he called and they again talked for hours while she excitedly primped and tinkered with her makeup, laid out her two outfits for the next day, and washed up. He stayed on the phone until her eyelids grew heavy and they said good night. He wanted his voice to be the last thing Michelle heard before she closed her eyes and fell asleep.

Lindholm Ranch
Rubidoux, California
April 18, 2001, 2:45 a.m.

Detective Welch was the newest detective, so he had the worst car. The department had assigned Welch a burgundy Buick Regal, the final survivor of a prior fleet purchase, as his unmarked detective unit—although Welch often used a pithier phrase to describe it. A few hard years had left the engine dogging on the slightest incline and one speaker had long since fallen out, causing the interior side panel to flop around whenever he opened the door. It was a cold night, so Welch sat with Knudson in his Taurus. Knudson's heater worked.

After the shock of viewing the tack room came the tedium of waiting while the forensic techs took photographs, measured, and bagged and tagged the evidence. Following the walk-through, Sergeant Mokar cut Deputy Barajas loose, then he held a briefing outside the front gate to assess the information they had so far. The man and woman in custody had been identified as Michael Thornton and Janeen Snyder, and both suspects had demanded legal counsel and declined to be interviewed. A preliminary records check showed that neither of them had ever been convicted of a felony, nor were they on parole. What they were left with was two suspects who wouldn't talk and an injured or deceased person who was still missing. The answers to their questions, no doubt, lay in the evidence at this crime scene and within the Suburban.

Mokar, Brown, and Garcia left after the briefing, but Welch and Knudson remained posted outside the Lindholm property to wait for the forensic techs to wrap up the crime scene. The department had sent over another forensic tech and both techs were photographing the ranch, first with photos showing the overall area and then zeroing in on each item of evidence in relation to its surroundings exactly as they had found it. Next they would take measurements showing the relative length, width, and height of each building, the distances between items of evidence in relation to fixed structures or other objects, such as fences. They also marked the locations of fences and the corral, made note of the surfaces, such as grass, gravel, blacktop, or dirt, and the location of the horse trailer and the vintage VW. After everything had been photographed and labeled, they would pick up each item and place it in a marked evidence bag labeled both with a number and a bar code. Evidence collection included taking lifts of fingerprints and shoeprints and the collection of biological evidence, such as blood and hair. They would also collect sample hairs from the horses Rocket and Dusty, the dogs Zachary and Sparky, and Kisser the barn cat. It was not necessary from a legal standpoint to collect all of the blood in the tack room and the breezeway, so the forensic techs would take representative samples. The tread marks on the driveway, in the dirt, and on the laundry from the clothesline would also be photographed as evidence. Given the size of the ranch and the amount of evidence strewn around the property, the forensic techs wouldn't begin collecting the items until close to dawn.

Inside the Taurus, Welch and Knudson revved up the heater in the early-morning hours and made use of their downtime. Welch worked on paperwork from the crime scene in Monique Bihm's garage while Knudson checked in with his wife, who had just processed their newest inmate, Janeen Snyder. Welch finished his report as Knudson pocketed his cell phone. Welch was sketching a rough diagram of the crime scene for his report and he was asking Knudson some questions. While they were talking, Knudson mentioned what he'd heard from Patti.

"That gal we arrested tonight had an ID on her with this kid's name on it," Knudson told him. "It was a health card from Las Vegas."

"What's the name?" Welch asked. As a teenager, he'd had to sit through a safety video to get a health-and-safety card in order to serve food at a burger joint.

"Michelle Leann Curran," Knudson said. "She also had a key to a Motel 6. Mokar said someone will run it down tomorrow."

"Why can't we do that now?" said Welch.

He was bored and antsy and didn't want to wait around if something could be done now. He knew he was supposed to listen, learn, and keep his mouth shut, but he was curious about the photo ID and the motel key and wanted to make calls while he did paperwork. He radioed dispatch and asked if someone there would check if the name

Michelle Curran matched a missing person in the Las
Vegas area. He was also curious about the motel keys
found on both suspects. Each of the locations—the Lindholm ranch, Jurupa Valley Park, and the Loring Ranch
neighborhood—were within a mile or two of one another.
The closest Motel 6 was on Valley Way, less than three
miles from where they were.

Within a few minutes, the dispatch called back with
confirmation that there was a missing person by that
name from the Las Vegas area. Welch thanked them and
called Las Vegas dispatch. They took Welch's information and promised to call him back when they got contact
information.

Well, that changed things, Welch thought. We have
this bloody barn, no body, a hotel key, and a missing juvenile. Someone is dead or close to being dead. We have
no idea how many intruders there were or how many cars
they drove onto the property. The existence of a second
vehicle at the crime scene would explain the lack of a
blood trail and could also explain why they had been unable to find the person they believed had been shot in the
tack room. None of the local hospitals had reported treating anyone for a gunshot wound after 4 p.m. Was an injured person taken to the motel room?

Welch phoned Sergeant Mokar and ran down his scenario. The link to a missing juvenile made an urgent
argument to do a welfare check of the room at the Motel
6, and Mokar gave Welch a green light. He reminded him
to take a sheriff's supervisor and a uniform, standard
procedure when police need to enter private premises, including motel rooms, without a search warrant to perform a welfare check. The law allows a cursory check for
a missing person, not a prolonged search. Happy with the
mere potential of a lead, Welch hustled to his burgundy
Buick and got back on the phone to ask the graveyard
shift patrol supervisor for a uniform and a supervisor to
meet him at the Motel 6 at 6830 Valley Way in Rubidoux.

It took Welch about five minutes door-to-door to get

from the Lindholm ranch to the motel, a dreary, two-story building that sat one gas station and a parking lot away from Route 60. The parking lot ran the length of the motel in front and there were extra-long spaces on the side for long-distance truckers to park their rigs. Welch arrived first and parked in front. He removed his suit coat and pulled his raid gear out of the trunk: a bulletproof vest, his duty belt, and a nylon windbreaker with "POLICE" on the back. The deputy and supervisor showed up a few minutes later, and he briefed them in the parking lot before they approached the office and told the night clerk why they were there. The clerk confirmed that "Crystal Snyder" and "Mike Thorn" were registered there in Room 210, up the stairs and around the back. Welch was excited that his hunch paid off. The clerk handed him the pass key.

The circumstances for entering the room met the textbook prerequisites for a high-risk forced entry—a large amount of blood at a crime scene, armed suspects and a missing juvenile. As they approached the room, they used flashlights to steady their service weapons and to flood the small room with light. Welch and the uniformed deputy used a classic cross-pattern entry with Welch taking a position on one side of the door and the deputy, crouching to avoid the window, on the other side. The position allowed them to cover each other from opposite angles of the small room once the door was opened. Using a regulation knock-notice, the supervisor called out, *"Sheriff's Department, open the door!"* and then used the pass key to open the door, making certain it swung open quickly and hit the wall to ensure no one was hiding behind it.

The room was quiet and unoccupied. Welch could easily see most of the small room once the door was opened. They quickly checked the bathroom and closet area, behind the shower curtain, in and under the unmade bed, and around the tiny desk and chair. They looked for blood or bandages in the sink, shower, toilet, bed, floor, and carpet and found none. There was no evidence that a severely injured person had been in the room. Welch noticed that the un-kempt motel room looked a lot like the Suburban. Clothes, shoes, and plastic food wrappers had been flung every-where. Once they found the room empty, they left quickly to avoid legal complications. Welch asked the supervisor to post a deputy at the front door to make certain that the motel maid didn't clean the room, and that no one dis-turbed the evidence until he could get a search warrant. One item in particular caught his eye: there was a pair of soaking wet blue jeans on the desk.

It was approaching 4 a.m. when they left the Motel 6. Welch phoned Mokar from the parking lot to let him know what he had found and ask what he should do. Mo-kar congratulated him and told him to return to the sta-tion to write up a search warrant for the motel room. And while he was at it, he could write up a warrant for the Suburban, too.

As dawn approached, Welch got a call from Las Ve-gas dispatch. They had a phone number for Candi Cur-ran, the mother of the missing girl, who had reported her daughter missing at 10:14 p.m. on April 4. It was 5:40 a.m. when Welch dialed the number. A weary-sounding Candi Curran answered.

"This is Detective Steven Welch of the Riverside County Sheriff's Department in California," he said. "Is this Candi Curran?"

"Yes, it is," she replied, sounding tired, but surprised and a little hopeful.

"We have two people in custody here in California with your daughter's ID," Welch said. "Their names are Michael Thornton and Janeen Snyder, who is also called Crystal. Do you know either of these people?"

Curran said she did not know the couple. Welch asked about the circumstances of her daughter's disappearance and what she was last seen wearing.

"She had a dark blue T-shirt that had 'Independent' written across the front," Candi said. "She was wearing Bongo blue jeans and white Etnies sneakers."

There was no need to mention the horrific scene in the tack room. It was important to be as vague as possible when calling the relatives of potential victims. For all he knew, Michelle had been robbed of her purse and Janeen was using her ID.

Las Vegas, Nevada
April 4, 2001, 7:00 a.m.

"Why aren't you getting ready for school?"

Michelle had one eye on her makeup mirror and the other on her sister. Tiffani was still in her pajamas on a school-day morning.

"Grandma said I could stay home," Tiffani said.

Michelle stomped out of their basement bedroom and up to the kitchen.

"Grandma, why can't I stay home? Tiffani's staying home," Michelle said.

"You stayed home yesterday," Jackie said. "You have to go to school. Now go get ready or you'll be late."

By the time Michelle had gotten to bed the night before, she'd had to crawl over Tiffani, who had already fallen asleep. Tiffani was mad that Michelle had woken her up, and now Michelle was mad that she had to go to school and Tiffani didn't. She knew that Tiffani would be spending the day with her boyfriend. For sisters who were barely one year apart, Tiffani and Michelle were as close as sisters could be, fantastic friends and vehement enemies. Sometimes they had contests to see who could hit each other the hardest. Michelle had stayed home with Steve the day before because he had a cold. His mother picked her up and stayed home with the teenagers all day while they talked, watched TV, and hung out until it was time for Michelle's Sonic shift. The thought of doing math, English, and U.S. history for an entire day seemed like an eternity, particularly when she knew that Tiffani would be with her boyfriend. Michelle was not going to let this go. But this time, her teenage frustration was directed at her grandma.

Michelle may not have been a high academic achiever, but Jackie had seen her granddaughter demonstrate responsibility beyond her years. One of Jackie's good friends and a close neighbor, Helen, had been undergoing treatment for cancer. Helen was the grandmother of a member of Tiffani and Michelle's cabal. Michelle often dropped by Helen's house across the street to clean, do dishes, and help out with whatever Helen needed. If Michelle wasn't at home or with her friends, she usually could be found at Helen's house.

And just the past weekend, Michelle had left a party early to attend a Sonic burger training session for the rest of the afternoon. When she had come home the next night after working her first full shift, she had been ecstatic about bringing home eighty dollars in tips. To Jackie's surprise, Michelle had given her half of it. Earning one's first eighty dollars in cash was a monumental occasion for a clothing-and-cosmetics-crazed sixteen-year-old. Jackie had never asked her granddaughter for a penny, but that was Michelle. Jackie knew she had a good heart, but Michelle still needed to attend school, no matter how much she protested, particularly because she had missed the day before.

The argument went on for about twenty minutes. It was not fair, Michelle argued to her grandmother. She wanted to stay home, too. If Tiffani got to stay home, why couldn't she? No, Jackie repeated. Michelle raised her voice at her grandma, loud enough for her uncle Bill to hear it as he got ready for work. It was a typical fit from a typical sixteen-year-old girl, but Grandma held her ground.

Michelle finally left the house at around 7:30 a.m. She was already late for school and would probably be even tardier because she told Tiffani that she planned to stop at McDonald's to pick up breakfast. She made sure everyone knew she was leaving because the slamming door resonated through the small house. Both girls had a flair for drama and said things out of anger that they didn't mean to one another or to their grandma, just to make them mad. That seemed to be the intent when Michelle stormed out of the house yelling, "I hope I get kidnapped and raped."

Lindholm Ranch
Rubidoux, California
April 18, 2001, 10 a.m.

Deputy Michael Angeli crawled on his hands and knees through the grassy horse pasture, looking. He scoured every inch of the front lawn, pored over the tool shed, and checked the roof of the house inch by inch. Angeli's painstaking examination of the Lindholm ranch, which had already been searched with a fine-tooth comb by a team of detectives and trained forensic technicians, appeared odd, but Angeli was looking for clues that the average person, and even the average deputy, could miss. Angeli approached crime scenes with the eyes of a trained hunter and tracker. He noticed how stalks of grass were bent, whether leaves and branches had been broken, and noted the composition and condition of soil. Angeli observed whether the soil had been freshly tilled or compacted and whether plants had been bent or replaced, which could be a signal that someone had buried a body. He looked for shoeprints, unusual patterns in the grass, leaves, and plants, and marks in the dirt, which would indicate that a body had been dragged.

Angeli had been notified of his assignment the night before, even as the detectives and forensic techs were conducting their meticulous, night-long search of the ranch. Collecting evidence in the dark was hardly ideal. Detectives Garcia and Brown wanted another pair of trained eyes on the crime scene in full sunlight to make certain they had not overlooked anything, and Knudson fully agreed with the idea. Angeli arrived at the ranch shortly after the forensics van had been driven away, stuffed with evidence. He had stopped by the station to pick up his collection kit, change clothes, and attend the briefing before heading to 46th and Riverview.

Frustration with the case spilled from the brass down to the uniforms and back up again. The supervisors wanted to make certain that they were covering each crime scene as well as their own backsides, particularly after the hours-long delay from CHU. They arranged a briefing for the case, separate from the standard patrol briefing for the morning shift. As if pressure from the case wasn't already dripping down the forehead of every station supervisor, the link to a missing juvenile substantially raised the stakes. A wave of secondary searches had been organized, with a team of deputies fanning out over the path of the chase in the Loring Ranch neighborhood to hunt for additional clues. A detective and a forensic tech had executed the search warrant on the Suburban, and would begin dissecting the vehicle soon. Still another team would tackle the motel room. If the sheriff's department couldn't find a body, the district attorney's office could not legally charge the two suspects with murder, nor would the DA be able to explain to a judge why the suspects shouldn't be released on $15,000 bail, the maximum for burglary. The case seemed more confounding in the cold light of day. Everyone knew that something had happened but they couldn't yet piece together what. Or who had been the victim.

Angeli had been a sheriff's deputy for twelve years and owned an outdoor gear store that serviced search-and-rescue teams and devoted backpackers. He served a unique dual function at the department. He was one of eight members of the Community Action Team (CAT), which identified issues in troubled neighborhoods that were not addressed by traditional law enforcement, then used creative approaches to help communities tackle those problems. When the need arose, he occasionally was pulled away to lend his expertise to cases where his centuries-old skills sometimes trumped the latest breakthroughs in forensic technology. Few people in the department could interpret a bent blade of grass like Angeli.

Angeli had honed his skills as a youth growing up on the outskirts of one of the world's most populated urban centers. His family split their time between San Bernardino, which adjoins Riverside, and their 1,200-acre mining compound in the Owens Valley. He had learned his skills from his father, who was a hunter and miner, and from various people he had met over the years, and he honed them working with various search-and-rescue units. He spent copious amounts of time in the Lake Arrowhead area, a mountain community above San Bernardino, and the Sierra Nevada.

His experiences as a youth allowed him to see things from a unique perspective. What most officers saw when they looked at the community of Rubidoux was a neighborhood in transition, a transformation of once-verdant ranches to suburban developments in economic peril and, more recently, the community's efforts at urban renewal. Deputies who cruised those streets saw high minority neighborhoods, homegrown fast-food joints, and modest homes next to well-manicured, old-money estates. Next to mini-malls spray-painted with graffiti, the homeless lived in cardboard boxes just blocks away from manors of the privileged.

When Angeli looked at Rubidoux, he saw Mount Rubidoux, which separated downtown Riverside from the town of Rubidoux. He saw the Santa Ana riverbed, a lush aquifer that made an oasis out of Rancho Jurupa Park. The 225-acre regional park and campground had a lake, waterways, miles and miles of bamboo, reeds, willows, and a veritable jungle that supported feral pigs, rabbits, coyotes, as well as a huge homeless population and the occasional methamphetamine lab. The perfect place, Angeli believed, for a body dump. It was just a half-mile from the Lindholm ranch. The same source of water that made Rancho Jurupa Park a verdant playground bordered the Lindholm ranch, fueling its lush greenery.

While he was at the station, he had changed into what was called battlefield dress, heavy military cargo pants and boots, and picked up his day pack, which had his fingerprint kit, gloves, and evidence collection bags. He met a still fearful Diane Lindholm at the front gate, who was fighting physical and emotional exhaustion as she once again found herself escorting a member of law enforcement around her property. Angeli's charge was to find any items that were out of place and, unlike Knudson and Clark, Angeli had the homeowner by his side to let him know what did—and didn't—belong there. His other charge was to document and diagram the blood in the tack room. Lindholm carefully walked the property with Angeli, then left him to his task, and returned to a neighbor's house down the street.

Angeli divided the property into a four-part grid: northeast, northwest, southeast, and southwest. He started at the northeastern corner of the ranch, an undeveloped field containing brush and vines and a horse corral, but the search yielded nothing noteworthy. Angeli moved on to the southeastern and the southwestern quarters, covering the pasture, vines, and densely overgrown brush that extended to the fence line inch by inch. He found nothing of significance and Lindholm had not identified anything unusual or out of place on their walk-through.

By afternoon, Angeli dug into the northwestern portion of the property, which included the front gate, lawn, driveway, tack room, tool shed, and house. He searched the roof, a popular place for suspects in flight to chuck evidence, but it yielded nothing but a wayward Frisbee. On the front lawn, Angeli collected the closing mechanism for the gate but didn't see the sunglasses that had been lying in the yard earlier when he walked through with Lindholm, and wondered whether Lindholm had inadvertently picked them up. On one side of the horse trailer, Angeli found a printed fee schedule for Rancho

Jurupa Park, where Janeen was arrested. The sheriff's
dive team already was organizing a search of the pond
and other waterways deep enough to conceal a body.

Like Knudson and Clark, Angeli saved the tack room
for last. On the concrete pad outside, the officer found a
pair of size 34 men's boxer shorts that Lindholm had said
didn't belong to her boyfriend or son. Angeli was unaware that the boxer shorts had vanished from the tack
room area the night before. He picked up the mug of pens
sitting atop a five-gallon plastic container and booked it
into evidence because Lindholm had said that she had
not placed it there.

Then Angeli entered the tack room. He took one look
around and saw the dried blood sprayed on the walls and
clinging to every corner of the room. The copious amounts
of the blood splatter, dried to a rusty-brown, would take
some time to document. Lindholm had told Angeli that a
number of items had been moved, including a blue plastic
electrical box that had been tacked to the wall, a soiled
white towel with red lettering still lying damp in the corner,
and Lindholm's uncle's anvil, which had been found upside down and was coated with a brown, sticky residue
that resembled blood. Angeli picked up a small piece of
crumpled gray duct tape, as well as a roll of duct tape and
a bottle containing plastic zip ties that Lindholm said had
been moved. He also collected a multicolored knit blanket, damp with blood, that Lindholm said did not belong
to her. When he finished diagramming the blood evidence in the tack room, Angeli turned his attention to the
peculiar rope contraption. The term "tack" refers collec-
tively to the equipment worn by horses, such as saddles,
bridles, reins, halters, and harnesses. The tack had been
strung together with other unrelated gear.

The black-and-green rope was wrapped up and over
and back through what looked like a bicycle cable lock
with eyelets on both ends. Fastened to the other end was
another nylon strap and another green-and-black rope that
was connected to a metal bolt implanted in the wooden

center ceiling beam. Diane Lindholm had told him that the tack was definitely out of place. Angeli noticed that the assembly of ropes was solidly connected to the wall and was sturdy enough to bear weight. Unlike other deputies who had been in the tack room, Angeli was familiar with horse tack. As he unhooked the cables and ropes and stuffed the contraption into his evidence bag, he didn't know exactly what the suspects had done with the ropes strung up that way. But it had had nothing to do with horses.

Las Vegas, Nevada
April 4, 2001, 5 p.m.

The letter that Steve had written for Michelle during school sat, unread, in his backpack. He waited all afternoon for Michelle to return his phone call. As the hours passed, he grew more concerned. The young couple had never stopped talking or gone an entire day without seeing each other. Steve knew something wasn't right. He went to Michelle's high school to look for her, thinking she might be in detention or with friends, but he didn't see her or see anyone who knew where she was. Then he called Tiffani. She had been wondering where Michelle was but assumed that she was with Steve.

Once they realized that neither one of them had seen Michelle, Tiffani got on the phone with every friend she could think of and every family member, but no one had seen or heard from her. Candi Curran went to the McDonald's and Michelle's other fast-food haunts to see if anyone had seen her. Steve went with Tiffani and a few of her friends and walked the route that Michelle would have taken to school: down their street, parallel to the highway, through the parking lot by her aunt Kai's house, then across to the high school. It usually took between a half-hour and forty-five minutes. As darkness fell, there was still no sign of Michelle. Candi and Jackie were frantic because it was not like Michelle to leave without telling anyone. Michelle had been upset and angry when she left, but that didn't explain why she wouldn't have gotten in touch with Steve. They knew that Michelle understood the inherent dangers of the greater Las Vegas area and knew better than to pick up a ride with someone. Tiffani phoned their friends and the manager at Sonic to see if Michelle had been called in to work. She scanned her memory of the previous weekend at the party for other connections or clues, possible plans Michelle may have made for this day, and ran through the events of the previous weekend when they'd gotten together with friends on a rare trip to goof around on the Las Vegas Strip.

Steve was also racking his brain, thinking back to the day before when he had last seen Michelle. He went over and over again in his mind what they'd talked about and their plan for getting together the next day after school. His mother had made both of them promise to attend school the next day, since they had both skipped classes that day. He had gone to school and thought that Michelle did, too. She'd said she was going to call him after school so he could pick her up. He tried to think whether he'd done anything to make her angry with him, whether there was any reason she would want to leave, but he came up empty. They had not argued; in fact, their young relationship was blossoming and getting better every day. They had gotten to know each other, and over the course of about six weeks, they had built a strong bond. He fought to push away worries that something had happened to Michelle.

Though just seventeen, Steve cared for Michelle in a way that he had never cared for anyone before. When they'd first met, she was self-conscious about the scar on her lip and she used to cover it with her hand when they talked, but he would tell her to take her hand away. He told her that she didn't need to cover it. He loved the way that she just melted when he would tell her that she was beautiful just the way she was. He was attracted to her in a way that went beyond a mere physical relationship. Despite having had opportunities to be alone, they resolved to wait to consummate their intimacy. Michelle had told him that she felt the same way about their relationship. When he had used drugs with a friend in her presence, she'd told him that if he continued to do so, she didn't want to be around him. He quit the next day.

The more time he spent with her, the more his feelings intensified. They were happy together, and he felt like he always wanted to see her and be with her.

He realized that he was falling in love.

By 10 p.m., Michelle's family and friends had exhausted every avenue, and Candi called the police department to report her daughter missing. The police wanted to know when Michelle was last seen and how she had been dressed, so Candi turned the phone over to Tiffani, who told police exactly what Michelle had been wearing: a dark blue, short-sleeved T-shirt with "Independent" in Old English style lettering across the front; size 1 Bongo blue jeans; size 6 white Etnies sneakers; a black Dickies purse with a small Dalmatian stuffed animal attached to the zipper; an eighteen-inch silver chain; and a silver Relic watch with a purple face. Michelle had also recently changed her blond hair color to dark brown with red highlights. As Tiffani spoke to the police, Candi stepped outside to the porch to light a cigarette and try to calm her nerves. She couldn't swallow the lump in her throat, and hoped that any second Michelle would walk through the front door.

Motel 6
Rubidoux, California
April 18, 2001, 3:30 p.m.

Search warrant in hand, Detective Allen Paine and forensic technician Marixa Scott knocked on the door of room

210 even though they knew no one would answer. California law required a knock-notice regardless of whether a room was known to be occupied prior to serving a warrant. As they crossed the threshold, Detective Paine announced to the vacant Motel 6 room in Rubidoux that the Riverside County Sheriff's Department had a warrant to search the premises. A deputy had been posted at the door since Detective Welch and the night shift supervisor had entered the room twelve hours before. Welch had finished writing the warrant and presented it to a judge for approval before heading home to catch a few hours of sleep.

Paine, a veteran investigator who had handled and assisted with hundreds of homicides, knew they had found an empty room. He noted the fast-food containers and the suspects' belongings on the dresser, desk, and littering the floor. There were two beds, one made and another with the covers pulled back as if it had been slept in. Paine and Scott set about their work quickly, knowing that the room could yield clues about a missing juvenile's whereabouts. Scott took photos, and she and Paine took turns packaging the items of evidence in paper bags, then labeling the bags and creating lists to document the seized items.

On top of the bed furthest from the door was a blue Eastport backpack, so full that it bulged. It contained a laptop computer with cords and a mouse; gloves; a knife in a sheath with duct tape; and a notebook with what appeared to be a partial license plate number of "4 LWT," and handwritten notes "Yvette Perkins," "car," "W" and a slash, and "plate on back window," "mouse," and "looking." There was also a zippered nylon bag containing Tarot cards and a book, *The Tarot: The Traditional Tarot Reinterpreted for the Modern World*. On top of the desk Paine found a pair of black men's Levis that still felt wet and cold to the touch through his latex gloves. In one pocket Paine found Michael Thornton's wallet, which had his California driver's license, social security card, and an Arrowhead Lake Association Board operator's certificate. The wallet was wet, too.

In the other pocket of Thornton's pants was a gun. Paine, a range master and forensics firearm expert, recognized the .38-caliber Taurus five-shot, double-action revolver. It was loaded. Also on the desktop was a pair of black undershorts, which like the wallet and jeans, felt wet through the gloves.

Moving toward the dresser, Paine saw a bandana, a *Mademoiselle* magazine, and some paperwork, including an invoice to Motel 6, but not for the one in Rubidoux. This one was for Room 211 at the Motel 6 in Fontana and bore a registration date of April 12 and a departure date of April 13. The Motel 6 in Fontana was about eight miles from Rubidoux on the other side of the 60 Freeway. The invoice was in the name of Ernesto Rios. When Paine moved the women's magazine and the motel invoice, he spotted a Polaroid photo. Two girls, one with bleached blond hair, the other with dark hair and red highlights, were seated in the front seat of a car that looked like the Suburban. Paine held the photo up to the light. The sullen blonde in the passenger seat resembled Janeen Snyder. Paine recognized the dark-haired girl from the missing-person notice sent to their department by Las Vegas police.

"This looks like our victim," he said, pointing out the missing Las Vegas juvenile. He handed the photo to the forensic technician.

In the recessed closet area near the bathroom, Paine found a half-full white laundry bag about the size of a military-style duffle bag. Paine pulled out the clothing one piece at a time, looking for clothing matching the description of what the missing girl had been wearing when she disappeared. He saw a few items that would fit a person of smaller stature like the missing girl. About a third of the way down the bag, he saw something navy blue. A chill went up his spine as Paine pulled out the small, dark blue T-shirt with a Maltese cross and the word "Independent" on the front. The T-shirt, which had been stuffed down in the bag with the rest of the dirty clothes, had been specifically detailed on the face of the search warrant.

As he continued processing the room, Paine found a pair of binoculars and a Radio Shack walkie-talkie on top of the neat bed. On the bed closest to the door, Paine found a plastic yellow-and-tan tackle box with the lid open. Inside were two pipes—one intact and one broken—that could be used to smoke crack or methamphetamine. The box also contained a plastic container with a white, crystalline substance, ammunition and gambling tokens for the Main Street Inn in Las Vegas. Paine recognized the cartridges for a Luger .9mm and a .22-caliber rifle. At a minimum, Paine figured them for street-level narcotics dealers, but criminals often diversified. He had a pretty good idea why they picked up the girl. Perhaps they intended to rob a bank or a liquor store with the ammo and communications equipment.

When they were through with the search, they had compiled two bags of evidence. Search warrants in California are created with an original and three duplicates. Two are filed with the court, one goes into the police case file, and the last copy goes to the individual being searched. Paine left a copy of the warrant on the unmade bed.

From a law enforcement perspective, Paine knew this had been a productive search. As the father of daughters the same age as the missing juvenile, Paine found the items in the motel room terrifying, just as they would be for any parent. It felt menacing to hold the girl's shirt in his gloved hands, knowing that she had been in that motel room, and to know that the people responsible for the girl's whereabouts had taken her picture. He hated to think what had happened to that little girl.

It had taken Paine and Scott a couple of hours to search the motel room. The suspects' Suburban, however, consumed the better part of the day for Detective

Carla Gordon and two criminalists. The brown Suburban was piled high with the suspects' belongings from the rear bench seat all the way to the doors at the back. Gordon glanced through the windows to get a feel for the items and created several categories in which to organize the volume of evidence. She labeled evidence boxes: tools, bedding, clothing, paperwork, camping equipment, and miscellaneous. The categories didn't include the guns, ammunition, and related firearms paraphernalia. The rear cargo area had a Winchester 12-gauge shotgun, a Colt .32-caliber six-shot revolver, a Western Field 410 Bolt-action shotgun, and a Remington 12-gauge shotgun, all of which were loaded. An H & R Arms .22-caliber nine-shot revolver was in a bag in the rear passenger seat. Boxes of ammunition for each weapon were stacked in the back. Maps, motel and store receipts, handwritten notes, checkbooks, vehicle registration, and bank paperwork was piled in various spots around the vehicle. She also found items typically used for surveillance and restraint: three sets of binoculars; a hundred-count package of cable ties; various lengths of clothesline and nylon rope; several bungee cords wrapped and knotted together; a knife with a round-shaped grip and duct tape stuck to the blade; bolt cutters; another wadded mess of nylon and Velcro straps; pieces of duct tape with strands of hair hanging from the tape; still another bundled ball of various cords and cables intertwined with a zip tie and a leather strap; and more rolls of duct tape, some dotted with long strands of hair. The paperwork would merit further investigation, such as numerous business cards for various hair salons in the Riverside area called the Fixx. The vehicle's title document bore the name Michael Thornton with an address on Silver Circle Street in Rialto, a nearby town. Gordon also saw references to at least two other homes, one in Arizona possibly belonging to Thornton's mother, and receipts for motels throughout the southwestern states, including Southern California, Nevada, and Arizona. A preliminary look at the documents indicated that Thornton and Snyder alternated between the home in suburban Rialto, a cabin in the ritzy, resort town Lake Arrowhead, and still another vacation home in the mountain town Running Springs, in addition to frequenting the motels.

But it was what Gordon saw in the front passenger seat that most caught her eye—a torn half of a green tank top with spaghetti straps, size 1 Bongo blue jeans, white Etnies sneakers, and a wallet with a social security card for Michelle Leann Curran.

Riverside Superior Court
April 19, 2001, 2:30 p.m.

An arraignment is a routine court appearance, as perfunctory as it is brief. The district attorney reads the charges in precise legal terms, and the defendant enters a plea, either guilty or not guilty. If a defendant can't afford legal counsel, the judge will appoint one, usually a public defender. Michael Thornton and Janeen Snyder had been arrested for garden-variety residential burglary, which carried a maximum bail of $15,000 apiece. Thornton and Snyder had been using a pay phone at the jail to call friends and given them their bank account access codes to withdraw money for bail. A couple of those friends, however, had second thoughts. They called police and spoke to Brown. With information they provided, Brown estimated that the defendants had well over $200,000 in their accounts and planned to post the combined $30,000 bail in cash. But the friends had another reason for calling police. Thornton and Snyder had entertained them with stories about kidnapping and murdering people, claiming that they chose victims who wouldn't immediately be missed, like runaways or hitchhikers. Their friends had dismissed the tall tales but were shocked after the couple was arrested and under investigation for a possible murder. They wanted to help police keep Thornton and Snyder in jail until it got sorted out.

Brown knew that the defendants could be released on bail unless they faced more serious charges that carried a higher bail. But they couldn't charge the defendants with murder or attempted murder until they found the body.

Brown and the other detectives knew that they didn't yet have the full story about what had occurred in the tack room. So when he showed up at Thornton and Snyder's arraignment, he brought along a legal surprise. It was a two-page form called a bail enhancement, which provides law enforcement a tool under section 1269 of the California Penal Code to present evidence and request that the judge set a higher bail than what's on the schedule. In the bail enhancement, Brown summarized the evidence the detectives had assembled so far: the large amount of arterial blood at the crime scene; the attempt to hose off the scene and wash evidence from their clothing; the ID of a missing Las Vegas juvenile found in Snyder's possession; the photograph of the missing girl with Snyder in Thornton's Suburban; the girl's "Independent" T-shirt in the Motel 6 room; and confirmation from Las Vegas that the missing girl had not been found. Brown included statements from the couple's friends that they had access to funds in excess of $200,000 in order to make bail, and pointed to their previous attempts to flee, and the fact that they had run in separate directions.

Brown sat at the prosecution table and waited for the judge to call the case. Michael Thornton and Janeen Snyder were ushered into court for their arraignment and sat in the jury box wearing orange jail jumpsuits and hopeful expressions, fully expecting to enter not guilty pleas to the burglary charges, post bail, and then walk away in civilian clothes. Brown waited while the judge handled other cases and kept an eye on the defendants, as he typically found it useful to observe defendants during their court appearances. Michael Thornton appeared calm and collected as if being arrested and locked up in jail were merely an inconvenience. Janeen Snyder, on the other hand, acted like a wide-eyed innocent, but Brown soon saw her other side.

The deputy district attorney dutifully read the charges of residential burglary, and Thornton and Snyder entered their not guilty pleas. The judge accepted the pleas and then took up the bail enhancement: "I'm going to grant the 1269 motion," the judge said. "Bail is set at $1 million."

Brown was relieved. He had asked for $500,000 apiece, but the judge raised it on his own. If these defendants wanted out, they'd need to pony up $250,000 to a bail bondsman.

Thornton maintained a blank expression, but Snyder's face darkened. She turned to look over at Brown, sitting at the prosecution table. In twenty-five years of chasing criminals, Brown had had his share of suspects give him hard looks in court, but he found Snyder's dead-eye stare unnerving. He instinctively glanced at the bailiff to see if he was paying attention, then looked back to Snyder. If looks could have killed him, hers would have. Now it was time to determine whether any of their stories would turn out to be true.

Three

Robert Presley Detention Center
Riverside, California
September 2002

For eighteen months, Michael Thornton got meals through a slot in his cell door in the county jail's high-power unit, where he was locked up nearly twenty-four hours a day with a cellmate who threatened physical violence if Thornton didn't stop talking. Thornton was driven to chatter constantly, an endlessly gushing spigot of venting, social and political commentary, idle chatter, and observations of whatever he was doing at the moment. Finally silenced by a younger and stronger adversary, the middle-aged and increasingly pot-bellied Thornton made the guards the unsuspecting recipients of his frenzied oratory; they were his sole source of human contact. He incessantly wrote letters to Snyder, confined in the women's section of the jail several floors up in the same eight-story building, plotting their defense strategy.

Inmates assigned to the high-power wing of the jail, also known as keep-away, wear red identification bracelets.

The most secure section of the jail, it is reserved for the unruliest of inmates, and for the ones most vulnerable to being attacked. When inmates arrive at the jail for booking, they are screened by the deputies to keep certain populations separate for the safety of the guards and other inmates. Members of rival gangs, for example, are assigned to separate units of the jail to avoid unnecessary altercations. Some inmates, such as suspected child molesters, police officers, celebrity defendants, and self-declared transgender and gay inmates, are typical targets for violent assault by other inmates.

As the months rolled on, Thornton heeded the advice of his lawyer about obeying the rules and following the guards' orders. When Thornton's attorney formally requested that Thornton be moved out of the high-power module, his behavior as a model inmate was taken into consideration and the housing order was granted. His near-solitary confinement at an end, Thornton received a new blue-and-white wristband for inmates housed on the third floor in protective custody (PC), the next lower level of security. The PC section of the jail contained four separate two-tiered pods of cells housing between forty and sixty inmates. The inmates of each PC unit are allowed contact with others within their unit, but are not allowed contact with any of the other three PC units, or with the general inmate population, also known as mainline.

At staggered mealtimes, the doors to the top and bottom tiers of one unit are open electronically to prevent even visual contact with inmates assigned to other PC units.

The grinding of heavy metal doors against the grate echoed through Cell Block 3B as inmates flooded the hallway and headed downstairs to the day room. Thornton hesitantly stepped out of his new home, Cell 3B67, as the door slid open. Jason Rea, a resident of the adjoining cell, 3B68, saw Thornton looking around. Having been in custody for just one week, Rea, thirty, saw that his new neighbor was unfamiliar with the routine as Rea had been.

"Chowtime," Rea said to him.

Thornton looked up and Rea walked him from their cells on the upper tier down the stairs to the day room. Once dyed black, Thornton's hair had grown out to a salt-and-pepper color and his gaunt frame had softened into the rounded physique of middle age after a continual diet of carbohydrate-rich jail fare. Breakfast came at 6 a.m. sharp, lunch was at noon and dinner was between 3 and 4 p.m. Rea and Thornton chatted as they stood in line to get their plates, then Rea walked Thornton to the far end of the dayroom and directed him to sit on the floor. There was no point looking for an empty seat at one of the tables. By the time the inmates from their section on the upper tier of cells got downstairs, all of the tables were crowded with inmates from the bottom tier who had arrived ahead of them, so Rea and Thornton ate sitting cross-legged on the floor.

"What are you in here for?" Thornton asked. Rea wasn't a longtime inmate, but he knew better than to ask another inmate that question. It was a time-honored rule that inmates don't ask each other about the criminal charges they were doing time for or for which they're awaiting trial. Rea had been a Volvo-driving, bottle-and-can recycling yuppie with a college degree whose discovery of methamphetamine in his late twenties quickly consumed his life. When his bank account was drained, he turned to writing bad checks and landed in jail. Rea, a Catholic and former altar boy, was ashamed of how addiction had turned his life upside down and wanted to use his jail time to straighten out. Though Rea hadn't yet been sentenced for his crimes, he hoped that he would be allowed to serve only a few months in jail in exchange for a guilty plea. By his attorney's estimate, Rea would be released by next spring, and he resolved to never again see the inside of a jail cell. He didn't mind sharing this information with Thornton, but he decided not to ask him about his case because he didn't care to find out whether Thornton was testing him.

Something about Thornton intrigued Rea, but he couldn't put his finger on what it was. Rea and Thornton had neighboring cells and neither liked their bunkmate, so Thornton and Rea started hanging out together, eating together, and playing cards. There was no doubt that Thornton had more than a year's worth of venting to get out of his system, but Rea sensed that Thornton was keeping something else bottled up, and didn't know how to open up because he didn't trust anybody. No inmate wanted to be in custody; who didn't need a friend? Rea decided that whatever weight Thornton carried with him, Rea could be his sounding board and listen to him without judgment. Thornton had told Rea that he had endured a long stint in high power with no one to talk to for more than a year. Although Thornton's ramblings dominated their conversations, Rea sensed that he wasn't ready to share what it was that troubled him most. Not yet.

In the protective custody floor of the jail, each PC unit had its own day room but took turns using a gym with a basketball court and exercise equipment to prevent mingling with other inmates. Unless the facility was under a temporary lockdown in which they were confined to their cells, inmates spent most of their time in the day room. Inmates entered the day room through a sliding metal door that opened and closed electronically. To the left of the door was a long panel of one-way mirrored glass running not quite the length of the room where deputies sat at a table, controlled the door and observed the prisoners. Directly in front of the door was a group of eight tables with bench seats bolted to the floor. A large television set hung to the right of the door, high enough on the wall to escape most spitwads and other projectiles, like food and silverware. The large area behind the tables was empty space where inmates could walk for exercise. Thornton and Rea often paced the area behind the tables, making a circuit around the room, talking while they walked. The blue-and-white color of the wristbands was repeated in the day room; the shade reminded Rea of his grandmother's powder-blue 1965 Mustang. Thornton liked to sit at the far end of the day room just out of eyesight of the deputies sitting behind the one-way glass. Sometimes they played card games, like Hearts or Spades. Rea subscribed to both the *Riverside Press-Enterprise*, the local newspaper, and the *New York Times*, which were delivered by mail, and he shared them with Thornton. This impressed Thornton, who prided himself for associating with a fellow prisoner who was smart enough to subscribe to two newspapers. One day, Thornton brought a photo of a girl with him to the day room and showed it to Rea.

"Who's that?" Rea asked.

"That's my girl," Thornton said with a smile. "She's upstairs," he said, indicating the women's section of the jail that was several floors above them.

Thornton wrote a letter to Janeen Snyder almost every day, he told Rea, and Thornton began to share the letters from her with Rea. Snyder often decorated her letters with small drawings or cartoon figures. The outgoing and incoming mail for certain, high-risk inmates was opened and read by the deputies for security reasons, as was mail from friends or relatives from outside the facility, but it remained a highlight of most inmates' time in custody and provided them with an important link to the outside world. Thornton, as Rea found out, liked to game the system. He and Snyder use code in their letters to send each other secret messages. Each time they wrote a letter, they would use the first word on each page to create the message. Snyder, Thornton said, was his soulmate. They had a bond: they finished each other's sentences, fought for one another, and worked well as a team. During the time that Thornton was in high power, he and Janeen had exchanged hundreds of letters.

It was typically during their card games that Thornton opened up about his past. Thornton joined the Air Force at age eighteen. He was married at the time, and his wife, Leilani, quickly became pregnant. In 1973, he met Pamela Bivens, who was engaged to a friend, another airman stationed in Biloxi. Bivens was on an extended vacation to

Biloxi with her sister and her sister's husband so that she could see her fiancé. Her fiance introduced Bivens to his friends, Michael and Leilani Thornton, and they socialized frequently during her six-week stay. Months later, Thornton and his wife split up, and he was transferred to March Air Force Base in California. Once in California, he found Bivens's phone number in Santa Ana and called her to ask if she was interested in going out with him. As it turned out, Bivens was no longer with her fiancé, and she accepted the invitation surprised that Thornton had remembered her. He took her to a motorcycle movie. Thornton saw that she didn't care much for the movie, but she liked him and thought he was smart. When he and his wife ended their marriage, Thornton took custody of the baby, Michael Jr. He thought Bivens fell in love with the baby as much as with him. Within a week, she had moved in.

Bivens told Thornton that he was the kind of person that she wanted to spend the rest of her life with. Thornton thought Bivens was moonstruck by the baby, but that didn't seem so bad. While he worked twelve-hour shifts, his mother, Jean Evans, stayed with them for a while to help care for Michael Jr. Thornton was discharged from the air force in August 1974, and they moved to an apartment in Long Beach where he worked for an oil rigging company and Bivens worked part-time at a health food store, though she spent most of her time taking care of the infant. A year later, Thornton's ex-wife reappeared to ask for custody of her son, and she took Thornton to court.

The ongoing custody battles over the next couple of years wore Thornton down, and he finally moved Bivens and Michael Jr. to Anchorage, where he would have more of an opportunity to find work and, more importantly, could escape the reach of the court.

Thornton got work as a cook in a twenty-four-hour restaurant/grocery store, but with the scarcity of jobs in Anchorage, he could only find a part-time position. Finally, he asked Bivens to marry him, and they wedded on

February 17, 1977. Their daughter, Angela, was born on October 27, 1978 in Anchorage, but his wife was hospitalized for a week after suffering complications from the birth. She suffered from severe post-partum depression and didn't feel as if she could go back to work. She wanted to return to California and eventually left Thornton, taking their daughter with her, though she didn't take Michael Jr. because the baby wasn't hers. Three months later, Thornton followed his wife back to California with Michael Jr., but he moved into a separate apartment. They decided to live apart while they sorted things out and dated each other for a year in order to see the children. The couple reunited in early 1980 and moved into an apartment in Ontario, California. Pamela got a job as a grocery checker and Thornton was a stocker, but he wasn't satisfied with part-time jobs and was tired of working for someone else. He decided to take advantage of his veteran's benefits to return to school. He was good at science, and physics in particular, but after taking a few classes, he thought it would take too long for him to earn a PhD and he wasn't sure that he was cut out for an academic career after all. He started taking business classes and found that he had a knack for the subject.

As he worked his way through the curriculum, Pamela often stayed up late at night to help her husband with his homework. But it was while he was working on a class project that something finally clicked. The assignment was to create a fully operable business plan, including finding bank financing, researching a potential location, comparing the business idea with local and regional competitors, determining the market feasibility in that location, complying with mandatory state and local regulations, researching what was required for licenses and permits by state and regional regulatory agencies, and determining the availability of potential employees. The couple brainstormed and came up with the idea of starting a hair salon, which they didn't think would be too complicated or too expensive. As they worked together to

complete the multi-layered assignment, Thornton realized that he had a viable business plan and he and Pamela
decided to put it to work.

They encountered snags at every turn. Bank loan officers balked at their lack of business experience. Neither
of them had held a full-time position, nor had they ever run
a business. They had no managerial experience and had
never even worked at a salon. Commercial leasing agents
doubted their ability to operate a beauty salon when neither of them held a license in cosmetology from the state.
Driven to overcome the obstacles, the couple found a leasing agent who believed in them and located a promising
storefront in a suburban mini-mall. The Thorntons opened
their salon in the city of Rialto in 1986, when Michael Jr.
was in fifth grade and Angela in second. They named their
salon the Fixx, with the last two letters formed by a pair of
crossed scissors. It was true that neither Pamela nor Michael had gone to beauty school and neither was licensed
to cut hair, but they didn't have to be. As the owners, they
hired hair stylists and selected a line of affordable beauty
products to sell in the salon. Michael set up his laptop to
handle payroll.

After they opened for business, the couple managed
the salon, raised two children, and held down their respective part-time jobs. Thornton found that he had a
knack for the beauty business, and the salon prospered.
Within a few months, Pamela quit her job and stayed at
home to take care of Michael Jr. and Angela. After one
year, the salon was doing so well that Thornton decided
to open a second one. When they opened the new salon in
San Bernardino, about ten miles away, Thornton finally
quit his job at the grocery store.

Thornton enjoyed being his own boss and worked
harder than he ever did working for someone else. The salons were so profitable that they opened a third one, then a
fourth. They thought it would be a good idea for one of them
to get a beautician's license since they now were the owners
of a chain of beauty salons. Since Michael was spending all

of his time running the businesses, they decided that Pamela would attend beauty school and learn to cut hair. She attended classes for several months, and while she was practicing haircuts, perms and hair color, Michael had also been busy. In 1991, as Pamela was finishing beauty school and applying for her license from the state, Michael was about to open their fifth store. By 1994, the Thorntons owned nine salons and employed more than fifty hair stylists. Thornton's aptitude for physics and science served him well when it came to technology, as he taught himself to perform advanced tasks on his computer. He prided himself on keeping his salons current with required licenses and permits.

Thornton enjoyed managing the salons, but he liked making money even more. The salons were grossing more than $1 million a year. He bought a new GMC truck for Pamela, a Jeep Grand Cherokee for himself, a house in Rialto, and a cozy lakefront mobile home in the resort town of Lake Arrowhead. He also bought himself a boat that he kept docked at the lake and showered his children with toys, computers, and the latest electronic gadgets. A family man, Thornton took his wife and children on fancy vacations, ate out at nice restaurants, and remained close to his mother, Jean Evans, in Arizona and his sister, Ricky Jo Cartwright, in Oklahoma.

Rea wondered whether Thornton's passions for success and detail explained his obsession with winning their jailhouse card games. Rea usually let Thornton win, but when they played as a team against other inmates, Thornton devised a system to cheat by holding his cards with one, two, three, or four fingers to signal to Rea that the suit was diamonds, hearts, clubs, or spades. A right thumb under the cards told him the cards were low; a left thumb indicated a higher card. Thornton had to win, and if Thornton didn't win, he flew into a rage, yelled, pounded the table, and stormed off. Rea would wait for a while, then walk over to Thornton, try to calm him down, and apologize, saying that it was his fault for losing. Sometimes, Rea told Thornton, he just had a lousy hand. Life behind bars was stressful and some inmates handled it better than others. Thornton was accustomed to success. Rea understood that he was used to getting what he wanted, qualities that no doubt served him well when building his business.

Rea was amazed that, of all the unfortunate souls who land in county jail, he would meet a former supermarket grocery bagger who had created an empire that grossed more than $1 million a year. After Thornton revealed the details of his life Rea developed newfound respect for him. It sounded like Thornton had lived a fairy-tale life as a self-made millionaire. How had someone that successful landed in county jail? From what Thornton had told him, he had been a law-abiding citizen until . . . what, Rea wondered?

After several weeks, Thornton asked Rea for his help. He wanted to send a letter to Snyder's defense attorney, but since all of their mail was read by jail deputies, he wanted Rea to hand-deliver the letter in person after he was released from jail in the spring. Thornton's request seemed innocuous, and Rea told him that he would be happy to help out.

A few days later, Rea found himself sitting next to Thornton on a bus packed with other inmates bound for Riverside Superior Court. The jail kept a schedule of when each inmate was required to appear in court for pretrial motions, preliminary hearings, trial, or sentencing. The prisoners were pulled out of their cells early in the morning and loaded onto a bus to the courthouse where bailiffs herded them into designated cells in the lockup area behind each courtroom. Thornton and Rea were headed for the same courtroom where routine procedural matters were handled before cases were farmed out to an individual judge for trial. When it was time to enter the courtroom, a pair of sheriff's deputies arrived at Thornton's cell to fasten a heavy chain around his waist that was threaded through his handcuffs and a second chain that linked his ankles together and attached to the waist chain. Rea had seen the same set of heavy chains on inmates who were accused of the most violent offenses, as well as for those who were a flight risk.

Soft-bellied and balding, Thornton didn't seem to match either category. The deputies escorted the inmates into the courtroom; those in protective custody were assigned to the far end of the jury box. Snyder was also seated in the jury box, since she and Thornton were codefendants in the same case. Because these were pretrial court appearances, no jurors were present. Thornton introduced Rea to Snyder and they chatted as if they were sipping lattes at a coffee shop, ignoring the orange jail jumpsuits and heavy chains that clanked with their every move.

Rea's case was called first, and his defense attorney and the prosecutor both agreed to delay the trial so that they could work out a plea deal. It was the first time that Thornton and Rea had been present at each other's court appearances, and Rea saw Thornton nod his head slightly to acknowledge that Rea had been truthful when Thornton had asked about his case. When the judge called Thornton's case, deputies walked Thornton and Snyder to the defendant's table, then stood by while the deputy district attorney and the defense attorneys began arguing the motions. Rea fought to remain poker-faced as he heard references to the criminal charges Thornton and Snyder faced: murder, rape, and torture with special circumstances that could lead to the death penalty. So that was it, Rea thought, a bit unnerved as Thornton turned toward him and grinned.

Despite the extreme violence Thornton was accused of committing, Rea still considered him a friend. That Thornton stood accused of breaking the first commandment rang in Rea's head, but his strict Catholic upbringing had taught him not to abandon anyone in need, and Thornton surely was troubled. Rea had grown fascinated by Thornton's flaws and if Thornton chose to tell him something about the crimes, Rea would listen. It was not Rea's job to judge and some day he might need Thornton as an ally. After all, Rea's safety and survival behind bars depended on keeping a secret of his own.

Rancho Jurupa Park
April 19, 2001, 5:40 p.m.

Bloodhound Maggie Mae took a whiff of the clothes in the brown paper evidence bag and made a brisk U-turn as a processional of detectives, deputies, and forensic techs followed close behind. The dog trotted purposefully from their starting point at the entrance gate to Rancho Jurupa Park, then headed up 46th Street. Detective Steven Welch, at the tail end of the parade, jogged obediently behind Maggie Mae, who had been scented with blue jeans belonging to Janeen Snyder that Detective Allen Paine had found in the Motel 6 room. When the dog reached the intersection of 46th Street and Riverview Avenue, she turned on Riverview and headed straight for the Lindholm ranch, then entered an undeveloped empty lot off the main road. Once pasture, the field had been overtaken by native California scrub and tall brush. Maggie Mae slipped easily through the foliage while her law enforcement entourage tromped clumsily behind her. The dog meandered through the field, back onto the road, then returned to the field, which sat between the park and Lindholm's ranch.

Welch's quick search of the Suburban at Monique Bihm's house and Deputy Michael Angeli's painstaking grid search of the Lindholm ranch had yielded clues pointing investigators to Rancho Jurupa Park. When Detective Scott Brown interviewed park employees, he located Jennifer Hill, a clerk at the front entrance, a powerful witness who put the suspects and a teenager matching the description of Michelle Curran in the Suburban just hours before intruders left the bloody scene in the tack room.

On that Tuesday afternoon. Hill had been stationed at the kiosk at the front gate of the park. She distinctly recalled the brown Suburban with dark tinted windows and a middle-aged male driver and two younger women, who were all in the front seat. The driver had paid Hill the six-dollar fee for a day pass, and Hill had recorded the date and time—April 17 at 1:45 p.m.—taping the receipt to the front windshield. The man had asked Hill if she could direct them to somewhere "private," where they could be alone, away from the general public. Hill had obliged, showing the driver a quiet, out-of-the-way location on a park map. She told police that he was so "highly intoxicated" and agitated that his speech slurred to the point where she could barely understand him. Sitting next to the passenger-side window was a blonde between seventeen and twenty years old whom Hill described as "jumpy." Between them had sat a younger girl who Hill estimated to be about fifteen years old, with very dark hair and who was possibly Hispanic. In contrast to the fidgety couple, the younger girl had seemed drowsy and "spaced out"; she was staring straight ahead as if under the influence of a depressant. Hill had had a gut feeling something was wrong with the docile girl and she'd tried to catch her eye for a sign that she needed help but couldn't get the teenager to look her way. The girl had been wearing a T-shirt under a black, hooded sweatshirt, and her hair was pulled neatly into a bun. Hill had thought that the girl was too young to be off campus early in the afternoon on a school day.

Unnerved, Hill hadn't been able to put her finger on exactly what worried her about this teenager. She had hoped to jot down the license plate number of the Suburban but hadn't been able to make it out as it sped away from her booth. Instead, she'd written down the time, a description of the car and its occupants, and her suspicion that all of them were under the influence. She'd radioed for a park ranger to come to her booth, given the ranger her notes, and told her where in the park she had directed the man and the two girls. About fifteen minutes later, Ranger Rosalie Grindle had contacted her via radio to let her know that she had spotted the threesome talking near one of the ponds. The man had been speaking and holding a black book inches from the girls' faces, pointing to it with his index finger while the two young women were nodding their heads as if to agree with him. It had looked to Grindle as if he was preaching to them. Since they weren't breaking park rules, she'd left and reported to Hill what she saw. Grindle had looked for them later in the afternoon and couldn't find them.

Ranger Grindle had not been close enough to identify the man and the girls for police. Hill, however, immediately recognized Thornton from a photo lineup and provided a description of the blond female in the car, who police believed was Janeen Snyder. Most importantly, Hill thought she recognized Michelle Curran from her photo on the missing juvenile poster, making the encounter with Michelle Curran and both suspects in the Suburban hours before the incident in the tack room the most powerful evidence they had so far.

Armed with this powerful witness and the "Independent" T-shirt and the Polaroid photo of the girl that Detective Paine found at the motel, detectives believed they were closing in, fueling a frenzied push to find Michelle. After finishing one search, they started another. Teams of detectives, deputies, and dogs that had spent days combing the crime scene at the ranch and the chase route fanned out again.

That day the latest round of bloodhound searches started at the front gate of the Lindholm ranch with Welch, the other detectives, and dog handler Coby Webb. She scented the dog with the dark blue "Independent" shirt. The bloodhound took in the scent and dutifully went up the driveway straight toward the tack room. Since the dog, days before, had been distracted by the odor of cat urine on the property, Webb halted the search to avoid ruining the dog's ability to track for the rest of the day, day since there were other areas lined up for the dog to explore. They decided to try another location and left the Lindholm property for Rancho Jurupa Park. At the entrance to the park, they scented Maggie Mae with Thornton's jeans from the motel room, which had dried overnight in the evidence room. The dog immediately headed toward the interior of the park to the pond, which is where the ranger had seen Thornton pointing to the black book and talking with the girls. The dog hit on the pond and two or three places around the pond, and marked the area by standing and barking at the points where she identified the scent. She was unable to locate a weapon or the girl.

Even though search dogs had been through the ranch and neighborhood multiple times, deputies scoured every inch of the Lindholm ranch, individual backyards and greenbelt corridors in the Ruis and Osage neighborhoods, and the Santa Ana riverbed and surrounding fields and pastures. Using grid searches and perimeter searches the deputies used a scrimmage line formation and walked the areas shoulder-to-shoulder. They turned up coins, a ring, a silver necklace and earrings, a plastic vial of multicolored rocks, a small plastic bag of pills, and a Polaroid photo of a man's naked torso found half-buried in the dirt in a backyard on Osage Avenue. Neighbors said none of the items looked familiar.

More searches of the park were planned. The department was coordinating a search of the pond with its search-and-rescue dive team. Deputy Angeli was mapping out the miles of waterways in the park with another deputy who was also an outdoor enthusiast. Every inch of the Lindholm ranch had been searched and searched again, with deputies, detectives, and dogs.

By Sunday, searches of the Lindholm ranch tapered off. After a stressful series of events, Diane Lindholm looked forward to putting the constant disruption behind her and getting a jump-start on the new week. Preparing to transport a client's horse, she decided to clean some clutter from the horse trailer parked by the tack room. She reached down to open a small compartment near the front of the trailer where one could transport a saddle.

And screamed.

From beneath a red, white, and blue fringed saddle blanket, a pale hand with splintered red nail polish reached from underneath a red, five-gallon gas container. Within the hour, a flotilla of police officers, detectives, criminalists, supervisors, and the coroner descended on the Lindholm ranch. Yellow crime-scene tape again encircled the corrals, the tack room, the house, and the outbuildings. A suited law enforcement cluster stood in the driveway for the briefing. All of the detectives who had scoured the ranch down to each blade of grass looking for a victim scowled at the black horse trailer next to the tack room, wondering how they—and the bloodhound—could have missed such an obvious hiding place and cursing under their breath for not knowing that horse trailers even had such a compartment. The door to the small area was on the side of the trailer toward the front; the deputies who examined the trailer had only opened the large doors at the back where the horse enters. The operative assumption was that the girl in the horse trailer was the missing Las Vegas girl until her identity could be confirmed with fingerprints or DNA.

Detective Richard Zerkel from the Central Homicide Unit was the on-call deputy that weekend. Having processed an unrelated homicide scene all night until Sunday morning, Zerkel was at home sleeping on Sunday afternoon when he was summoned to respond to the Lindholm ranch. Though he was assigned to the CHU that was based in downtown Riverside, he was well aware of the peculiar case that had been vexing detectives out in Rubidoux all week. In fifteen years with the department, he couldn't recall a murder case in which the homicide scene had been processed and the prime suspects were already in custody before the victim was discovered.

The deputy who was the first to arrive at the Lindholm ranch after the victim's grisly discovery took the detectives on a now-familiar walk-through of the ranch. They headed up the driveway to where the black trailer was parked on a concrete apron next to the Volkswagen. The young girl lay inside, still covered with the horse blanket. After the walk-through of the crime scene, the supervisors left Zerkel with the forensic technician to process the crime scene—again. Zerkel knew that the entire ranch had been thoroughly searched at least three times, and was aware that no one had located the body or a murder weapon. For his purposes, Zerkel considered his crime scene to be not only the ranch as a whole but the saddle compartment itself, which had never been searched.

Zerkel and the forensic techs began with a perimeter search to take advantage of the waning daylight in hopes of finding a gun, knife, or additional shell casings or bullets. They performed a thorough grid search of the grassy areas, bushes, the stream that ran the length of the property, and the corrals, then worked their way through the outbuildings and the tack room. Zerkel knew this would be their last crack at finding evidence and he wanted to move every item in the tack room and physically examine them, including the storage boxes, the toys, the tack, and the saddles. Once Zerkel and the forensic techs started moving the boxes aside, they found a leather riding crop, bloodied and broken in half, lying next to a pool of dried blood caked on the cement. Zerkel found a nylon windbreaker and several pieces of bloodied duct tape. On the center roof beam were two posters, one of horses and the other of a tiger, both with globs of blood that had soaked through to the back. Moving the boxes revealed a floor littered with plastic cable ties in different colors, sizes, and thicknesses, and many were spotted with blood. In addition, there were several containers of a similar array of cable ties, some of which belonged to Lindholm and some that Thornton and Snyder had apparently brought along and left there. Zerkel noted the plastic zip ties on the victim's wrist and asked the forensic technician to collect all of them.

By evening, Zerkel was ready to examine the compartment containing the girl's body. Forensic technician Marixa Scott, who had helped Detective Paine process the Motel 6 room the day before, took photos, dusted the door and sides of the trailer for fingerprints, and measured the small compartment. It was three to three and a half feet wide, about three and a half feet high, and about two feet off the ground. The door opened sideways; a three-row caddy hooked to the inside of the door held cleaning supplies, rags, and grooming tools. With the door standing open, the girl's arm extended from underneath the gas can. Zerkel had to stoop over in order to see the back of the compartment where one could see her bare knees sticking out from beneath the blanket. Zerkel asked the forensic tech to remove and collect the gas can, which still contained liquid, and process it later for fingerprints. Next, he asked Scott to lift the blanket from the body and collect it as evidence.

With the blanket removed, Zerkel saw that the young girl's body was nude and lying in a contorted position, but it had not been flung with the typical thoughtlessness and haste that follows most murders. The victim had been bent backward in an exaggerated arch so that her head was folded underneath her body. Her chin rested on the floor and her feet and buttocks were above her head. Her buttocks sat on some plastic ice chests and a purple bucket. Plastic cable ties were looped around her wrist. Zerkel carefully studied the position and condition of the body and Scott took numerous photographs. When they had finished, the coroner's deputy gently removed the girl from the trailer compartment and placed her on a plastic collection sheet on a grassy area next to the trailer for photographs and preliminary processing. Several plastic ziplock bags and other refuse were stuck to her arm and hand. Forensic technician Paul Stamm knelt next to the girl's body and began collecting trace evidence, such as hairs, fibers, soil, and paint. He touched lengths of cellophane tape to each section of the girl body, working systematically. The tape from each section was then placed in a container resembling a plastic petri dish with the tape suspended inside the dish so that it didn't touch the lid, bottom, or sides when the top was screwed on.

Zerkel stood at the edge of the coroner's collection tarp to watch Stamm and study the marks and other evidence on the body. He noted two separate cable ties on the right wrist, one was wrapped tightly around the wrist and the second was looped through the first. The left wrist had a ligature mark matching the zip tie on the right. Both ankles bore similar ligature marks as well as a sticky residue, most likely from duct tape that had been wrapped around them. It looked as though she had a bite mark on her right calf, an abrasion on her right shoulder blade, and numerous dried blood smear all over her body. There was a single gunshot wound to the forehead, squarely between the eyes, that seemed to be the obvious cause of death.

Zerkel stepped over to the trailer and peered inside the compartment, which still held the bucket and the ice chests. The trailer floor contained the usual trace debris from hauling horses—soil, horse hair, and shards of hay. A few drops of blood speckled the floor under the area where the body had been propped up against the ice chests and the bucket. He saw bloody smears that looked like transfer stains where parts of the girl's body brushed against the inside trailer wall. The trailer showed no signs of having been washed down in the same way the intruders had hosed out the tack room. It seemed obvious to Zerkel that the girl had been shot and died in the tack room where profuse bleeding from the fatal head wound would account for the significant quantity of blood there. She had then been placed in the small trailer compartment.

Zerkel did not want to think about the situation in which Diane Lindholm found herself when she came home and heard the single gunshot that killed this girl.

Lindholm had been extremely lucky. After committing one murder, what would have stopped the intruders from committing another to silence the sole witness—the only person who could place Janeen Snyder and an unseen male intruder next to the tack room moments after a shot was fired? Lindholm had undoubtedly interrupted the killers in the tack room, accounting for the sheer volume of the suspects' personal items that were strewn across the tack room and dropped or buried along the escape route. The suspects had been spotted on foot by the police helicopter within minutes of Lindholm's 9-1-1 phone call.

The girl's unusual position in the trailer haunted Zerkel. How did she get posed as if she were doing a backflip? It was disturbing to Zerkel, a veteran homicide detective, that Thornton and Snyder couldn't find the time to gather the personal belongings that could link them to a heinous crime, and yet they took the time to remove the bindings from the girl's body, wash down the tack room, carry her to the trailer, and arrange her body in a sexually vulgar pose, as if leaving behind their signature or making a statement.

Hours later, an investigator with the Riverside County Coroner's Office determined that the remains were that of Michelle Curran. The information was immediately relayed to the Clark County Coroner's Office in Las Vegas, which sent a representative to the Curran household to make the death notification in person. Tiffani had been outside in the yard and saw a man drive to the house and knock on their front door. Within moments, she heard a loud noise and came into the house to find her mother, Candi, sobbing as she lay on the floor.

When news of Michelle's death spread through her high school, her classmates created a banner with messages and signatures. Tiffani and Candi taped up the banner in the basement bedroom and created a shrine to Michelle featuring her favorite cartoon characters, the black-and-white spotted puppies from the animated Disney film *101 Dalmatians*, and photos of Michelle laughing and smiling with friends. To help the family pay for burial expenses, the school held a car wash. Michelle's home economics teacher helped her students complete the Dalmatian puppy–themed blanket that Michelle had been sewing at the time she disappeared and presented it to the Curran family. Tiffani fastened the blanket next to the banner on the bedroom wall.

From the first night that Michelle went missing, Tiffani had to sleep alone in their bed every night, wondering where Michelle was, if she was safe, and when she was coming home. Tiffani found it hard to concentrate on schoolwork. Like the other members of her family, she was in shock. She asked her boyfriend to pick her up and take her to his house, since she could not bear to sleep in the same bedroom and in the same bed that she had shared with Michelle. Returning to her own bedroom reminded her that Michelle was gone forever. Tiffani felt responsible because Michelle might not have disappeared if Tiffani had gone to school with her that day. She regretted not telling her sister enough times that she loved her. She took small comfort in carrying around the small stuffed Dalmatian that Michelle cuddled up with when she went to sleep. Michelle had also carried a miniature Dalmatian on her key chain, which she had when she disappeared.

Tiffani could not wear the jeans that they had shared or the shirts they fought over, and she couldn't bear to look at the extensive collection of makeup that Michelle had spent hours trying on at various department store cosmetics counters. She didn't want to get her nails done because it reminded her of the first time she and Michelle had their first full manicures. They had nagged their Aunt Kai for weeks to do their nails. Finally, Kai had set aside the time and spent more than three hours on both girls applying acrylic nails and painting nail polish with French tips. When Kai finished, Tiffani and Michelle admired her work and Kai left the room for a few minutes. She told the girls that they needed to sit quietly for at least twenty minutes while their nails dried, but the young, energetic girls couldn't sit still. When Kai walked back into the room, the girls were gone. Tiffani and Michelle's turn at adulthood had been sidelined by youthful whimsy as the sisters attempted to turn the most cartwheels on the front lawn in spite of their still-wet, perfectly painted nails.

The discovery of a homicide victim typically unleashes a massive law enforcement machine to unearth evidence, witnesses, and the other clues to lead them to ensnare the perpetrator. In this case, the primary suspects were already in custody and investigators at the Jurupa Valley station had the incriminating evidence in hand that linked Thornton and Snyder with Michelle Curran's murder. On the Monday following the discovery of Michelle's body, the case unfurled in several directions. Detectives Garcia, Brown, Welch, Angeli, and Paine, with other investigators based out of the Jurupa Valley station, continued to follow leads, but they were now required to report to Detective Robert Joseph of the Central Homicide Unit in downtown Riverside, who was the case supervisor assigned by CHU. Joseph immediately ordered another round of searches covering the mile-and-a-half chase route between Lindholm's ranch and Monique Bihm's home, the route where the suspects had hosed themselves off and buried their personal belongings. The emphasis of the repeat searches was to locate the automatic weapon to match the .380 caliber shell casing found in the tack room, which they now knew had been used to murder Michelle Curran. Deputies, students, cadets, forensic ID techs and volunteers canvassed every possible route from Lindholm's driveway on 46th Street to Bihm's driveway at 4060 Ruis Court where the Suburban had been sticking halfway out of the garage. Joseph also ordered another search of the Lindholm ranch using dogs and metal detectors. They searched the area from Bihm's garage to the backyard where Thornton had been apprehended; the location where Snyder had flagged down the county worker in his truck; and the overgrown area around the Santa Ana River. Even after trying a variety of search techniques, including dogs, and metal detectors, they were unable to locate the murder weapon. On the bright side, the county worker later contacted sheriff's deputies to report that his uninvited passenger had left behind a keychain, which had an Etnies logo and a pint-sized, stuffed, black-and-white Dalmatian puppy.

While deputies searched the suburbs of Rubidoux, Detective Carla Gordon returned to the brown Suburban, at Detective Joseph's request, to sort through Thornton's and Snyder's personal belongings. The volume of personal items in the back of the Suburban filled the vehicle from the rear bench seat all the way to the doors in back. In some places, it was as deep as the base of the window frame and the top of the bench seat. Guns and ammunition were immediately removed and taken to a locked evidence facility. Gordon organized the remaining items into seven categories: paperwork, clothing, shoes, tools, bedding, coats, and miscellaneous items that didn't fit into the other categories. Forensic technician Rob Riedman took additional tape lifts of the carpeting, the upholstery, and the seats.

Detective Gordon found a variety of documents, including a notebook containing notes, receipts, and some nude photographs, including one of Snyder and Thornton, a photo of Thornton drinking, a payroll check dated February 2, 2001, for someone at the Fixx hair salon, and checkbooks for salons in Rialto, Riverside, and Redlands. As Gordon sorted the wads of receipts and bits of paper stashed in the Suburban, she separated a series of motel, restaurant, and retail store receipts corresponding to the days that Michelle Curran was missing and leading up to the date the suspects were arrested. There were receipts from the Lake Arrowhead Resort in California, from Motel 6 locations in several cities, and from businesses in Arizona and Nevada. Some of the paperwork also made reference to residences in Lake Arrowhead; Running Springs; Mesa, Arizona; and Rialto. The next of many investigative steps would be to trace the paper trail that Thornton and Snyder had left behind, following their footsteps through the days leading up to Michelle Curran's murder. Detective Gordon also found a Polaroid camera and a live .38-caliber bullet in the rear cargo compartment, a brown purse containing a monocular, an envelope labeled "My love's ponytail" with brown hair tied in a ponytail inside, a Nokia cell phone with the power-up message "I love you partner," a coin purse containing loose change, and a nylon bag containing miscellaneous ropes and cords.

Gordon made a note of the Suburban's features, including the fact that it had manual windows as opposed to power ones. As she examined each of the windows, she saw a slender piece of metal, like a large paper clip, lodged in the locking mechanism that jammed the door. With the clip in place, the door would not open from either the inside or the outside. Once Gordon removed it, the door was fully functional.

From a legal standpoint, the discovery of Michelle's body pushed the district attorney's office into high gear to file murder charges against Thornton and Snyder. Preliminary forensic tests revealed evidence of sexual activity and the district attorney's office charged both defendants with kidnapping and sexual assault along with homicide, leaving open the possibility that they could face the death penalty. Additional charges would be filed if the autopsy results showed that the defendants had committed other violent acts prior to Michelle's murder. As Joseph managed the case from his end, the investigatory arm of the district attorney's office sprang into action. The case was assigned to veteran district attorney investigator George Hudson, who had worked homicides and sex crimes, including those of high-profile killer and serial rapist Warren Bland and serial killer William Suff. Tall, wiry-haired, and still muscular even though nearing retirement, Hudson had a gentle demeanor that calmed victims, unnerved suspects, and veiled his fanatical persistence. A former deputy sheriff and homicide investigator, Hudson was known for taking cases from police agencies a step further by digging through defendants' past crimes and prior uncharged offenses. The introduction of this evidence can help build a case at trial if the incidents pass legal muster by matching the manner and pattern of the crime being charged or establishing a pattern. In this way, a prosecutor can create a fuller picture of their criminal history. The Thornton and Snyder case landed on Hudson's desk on Monday morning. By the afternoon, he was standing in the yard of the Lindholm ranch on Riverview Avenue with Detectives Brown and Garcia, looking at the layout of the property.

Hudson was an Old West enthusiast and a skilled horseman who was familiar with tack. When he saw photos of the tack room with the ropes and bridles strung up on the wall and the center beam and examined photos of the marks around the victim's wrists and ankles, his experience as a sex crimes investigator told him that the defendants had used the tack to somehow dangle their victim during the sexual assault.

What was still a mystery was the connection between the suspects and their victim. Michelle Curran was a schoolgirl from suburban Las Vegas. Thornton was a millionaire salon owner with several properties in Southern California. Bank records showed that he had a healthy six figures in his bank account. What was he doing with Janeen Snyder, a girl young enough to be his daughter? How had the two crossed paths with Michelle Curran? How did the victim wind up in Riverside, California? And where had she been for nearly two weeks?

Hudson's inquiry dovetailed with that of sheriff's department investigators in a search of the defendant's home—or in this case, homes. Welch had been asked to

write search warrants for all of the properties Thornton
owned. Property records indicated that he owned three
residences in Southern California: a home in the suburbs
of Rialto; a large, lakefront cabin in Running Springs;
and a smaller home in Blue Jay, which was one of the small
mountain communities nestled around the larger resort
area of Lake Arrowhead. Hudson accompanied detectives
from CHU and the Jurupa Valley as they moved from one
house to the next. They started with the home in Blue Jay,
which was located in a privately owned complex of mobile homes, the only such park in the exclusive resort area
of Lake Arrowhead where each home had a lakefront
view. Hudson happened to know the property manager,
Nick Fogg, who had been the boat mechanic for the sheriff's department's patrol boats in the 1970s when Hudson
had lived in the nearby Twin Peaks area.

The small army of detectives arrived at the park with a
team of forensic technicians and met with Fogg and the
park's maintenance man, Edward Bibb. Bibb told the detectives that Thornton had reported a break-in at his place
a month or two before his arrest. Bibb had photographed
the broken window and made a note of it in his maintenance journal for the property. He said that he would provide the detectives with a copy of the photos and his journal
notes from that day. Bibb also said that he recalled seeing
Thornton quite often with Snyder. He also recalled seeing
both of them many months before with a young red-haired
woman, though she didn't match the description of Michelle Curran.

The smallish home had fallen into disrepair and was
cluttered with debris. The detectives and forensic techs
photographed the home and hunted for anything that
would shed light on the relationship between Thornton,
Snyder, and Michelle Curran, or on Michelle's murder.

The team's next target was Thornton's cabin in Running Springs, which was several miles down the road
from the mobile home park. Set into the hillside, the tradi-

tional, light blue cabin was a spacious, multi-level home. From the street, one climbed a set of stairs to a latticed porch surrounding the front door. When investigators entered the living room, the first thing they encountered was a sofa and mattress in the middle of the room with ligatures on the rails of the bed. Photographs of women in various sexual positions were hung on the pine-paneled walls and a fluffy, white teddy bear swung from a noose. The wood walls and beamed ceilings bore a rich, dark stain, giving the room, with its graphic décor, a sinister gloom. On one wall was a handmade poster with cut-out newspaper headlines reading "KILLING," "EXCITEMENT," "SHOOTING," "DANGER," "TROUBLE," and "A DISHONEST MURDER." Red paint resembling blood was smeared between the cut-outs. Another poster comprised of newspaper headlines read "BUSINESS," "MONEY," "NO LIVING," "MORE PAIN," "NOW WE'RE EVEN." A "Certificate of Homicide" taped to the wall bore the moniker "Chris the Psychotic" and represented the completion of "Phase ONE of Uncle Rocky's School for HITMEN." A revised Serenity Prayer was also taped to the wall: "Lord, grant me the serenity to accept the things I cannot change, the courage to change the things I can, and the wisdom to hide the bodies of those people I had to kill because they pissed me off." Nearby was a cut-out newspaper clipping from a Tulsa, Oklahoma, newspaper with a 1996 dateline.

As the detectives systematically looked through the house, Welch saw something odd about the stairs leading down to the basement. He bent down to examine them and found many of the treads, the part of the stair that one steps upon, were loose. Welch removed the treads and shined his heavy-duty flashlight on the area underneath the steps, which were located directly above the hillside. He saw that someone had dug into the side of the hill to create a narrow tunnel. Once the treads were removed, the stairwell formed a walkway that gave way to a dirt tunnel that led left into a room that was also dug from dirt. Welch, now joined by other investigators, later admitted that his skin crawled as he followed the tunnel into the small room, which contained nothing but a mattress on the floor and a few chairs, all of which still had duct tape stuck to them. The investigators had little doubt that the room had been used as a torture chamber. Detective Welch and Investigator Hudson felt as if they had walked into the cabin of a modern-day Charles Manson. The investigators climbed out of the underground room and quietly gathered in the living room to discuss what they had seen. Next to where they stood near the fireplace mantle was a small poster that read, "The Dark Lair of Infinite Evil."

"I know Michael Thornton and Janeen Snyder personally."

The anonymous caller on the phone wouldn't give her name to the on-duty Riverside County district attorney investigator.

"I have information that they killed other people," the woman said. "There's more to this than you know."

The on-duty investigator conveyed the information to Hudson, who asked a forensic technician to perform a reverse trace on the phone number. Within a few hours, the technician told him that the call originated from a pay phone at a casino in Las Vegas. That was good news. Casinos have hidden cameras covering every nook and cranny, so it was probable that their anonymous caller had been filmed while using the phone. Hudson contacted the head of security at the casino, who confirmed that one camera remained trained on the bank of pay phones, one of which had been used to call the district attorney's office in Riverside. She agreed to pull the security video from the time the call had been placed and set it aside for Hudson, who could compare the time of the call with the security video in hopes of identifying the caller. At first glance, the casino security chief told

Hudson that the caller appeared to be an attractive young woman who had a toddler in a stroller with her when she made the phone call.

Hudson thanked the woman and booked a flight to Las Vegas.

Four

Beauty Killers

Robert Presley Detention Center
Riverside, California
September 2002

The first page of Thornton's letter was in his own penciled scrawl. "The following is reportedly the story given by Michael F. Thornton regarding his relationship with Janeen M. Snyder and the events surrounding the death of Michelle Curran. The author of this document can positively identify himself by use of the following number, 5064, but otherwise wishes to stay anonymous. No other copies of this document exist and it is intended for the above-named individuals only."

Rea didn't know where Thornton came up with the number 5064, and he didn't ask. Rea planned to lie low and serve his time so he could get out in a few months. He wanted to be a friend, listen to what Thornton had to say, and not ask any questions. He saw from the letters Thornton had received from Snyder that she was unsophisticated and seemingly lost without him. She wrote that she was "freaked out!" at the prospect of spending the rest of her life behind bars.

"Please do something to help me!" she wrote. "You've lived your life. I've never lived mine!"

Thornton wrote back to reassure Snyder that he was planning to take responsibility for everything. Using the secret code that they had worked out, Thornton told her that they could say the gun had been dropped on the tack room floor, or that it went off accidentally. He reassured Snyder that she shouldn't worry because he loved her more than anything and that he was working out their trial strategy. Ultimately, Thornton wanted to convince Snyder through the secret messages that he would testify and take the blame for shooting Michelle and spare her. Rea thought that was honorable. Snyder was young and had a life to live, and Thornton was well into his forties.

Thornton and Rea worked on the letter with renewed vigor. There wasn't a moment that they weren't with one another talking, eating, or playing Spades. The letter project was a bonding experience for them, but it was not mutually beneficial. Rea had hoped the months in jail would provide time for quiet reflection upon the poor choices he had made, but his new friend made that impossible. Thornton filled Rea's days with increasingly detailed accounts of his life, his hatred for his ex-wife Pamela, who had divorced him in 1999, and his love for Snyder. Thornton continued to share with Rea the letters Snyder wrote to Thornton from jail. A few of them were adorned with Snyder's drawings, like hearts, a bird or a sad hound dog sitting next to a mailbox.

"I remember all the fun time we shared, baby," Snyder wrote. "I (heart) you, always thinking of you."

Thornton gave Rea some of Snyder's letters for safe-keeping, but Rea wondered why he would do that. Inmates' cells can be searched at will by deputies, but once they find that personal letters contain no contraband or escape plans, they are returned. Rea thought that giving him the letters was Thornton's way of showing he was trusted enough to keep something he cared about.

As they spent more time together, Thornton started to exert control over Rea by disapproving when he socialized with other inmates. Rea saw this as an attempt to control with whom he spoke, perhaps in order to keep the letter project safe.

Thornton was adamant about how they should structure their defense. His idea was to spell out what he wanted Snyder to know about their strategy ahead of time. If Rea delivered the letter directly to Snyder's defense attorney, they could bypass the jail mail system, keeping it away from the prying eyes of deputies, and of course, the prosecution. The letter, Thornton said, would be "different from the truth"—it would be *their* truth, as dictated by Thornton. The letter would not be factual; it would be exactly what he wanted their story to be and exactly what he wanted jurors to hear. He needed Snyder to be on the same page so that their stories would match.

Over time, Rea saw several themes emerge. First, Thornton wanted it to appear as if anything bad that had happened was an accident and not intentional. Second, Thornton wanted his letter to become a moral tale against drug use by blaming his criminal behavior on his inability to think clearly because of his methamphetamine use. From his own experience with the criminal justice system, Rea knew that alcohol or drug intoxication or addiction did not constitute a defense to a criminal act—not that defendants don't try. Rea knew that Thornton was smart, but he didn't think that his attempt to use his drug use as a defense was very original, or would yield the results he expected.

Thornton wanted the running theme of the letter to be that he had really cared for Michelle Curran and had never intended to cause her any harm. He wanted the letter to state that he had always planned to give Michelle her own salon to run.

None of these things were true, Thornton told Rea, he just wanted them in the letter.

Las Vegas, Nevada
May 1, 2001

Investigator George Hudson, in his usual business attire, felt horribly overdressed as he made his way through the parts of a Las Vegas casino that most tourists rarely visit. The Maxim Hotel and Casino was undergoing a major remodeling, and he and Deputy District Attorney Michael Rushton made their way through construction debris and a staging area where performers wore barely a spangle. Hudson usually worked cases on his own, as he had for thirty years, but Rushton had wanted to tag along this time. Hudson could clearly see that Rushton, who had a deeply religious background, was a bit uncomfortable behind the scenes at Sin City. Clean shaven, with boyish good looks, Rushton had put on a few pounds as he entered his forties, though the undergarments required of strict Mormon practitioners, which he always wore, even under his suit, may have accounted for some extra bulk. Hudson showed the photo in the video to a few of the employees, who confirmed that the woman in the phone booth with a child in a stroller was a stripper at a neighboring casino named Angela.

Her full name was Angela Thornton.

Could this be Thornton's daughter? Hudson got a phone number from the security chief at the casino where she worked and called her. She acknowledged that she was Thornton's daughter and agreed to talk.

The next day, Angela Thornton greeted Hudson and Rushton at her apartment located a few blocks from the Strip. She made a good living as an exotic dancer and lived with the toddler's father, her childhood boyfriend, Allen Jiminez. She sat curled up on the couch, and Hudson, wanting to make her feel at ease, talked shop about her profession. Hudson often zeroed in on what relaxed victims and witnesses, putting them at ease by talking about something that felt normal for them. He did this with Angela, though he took notice of Rushton's growing discomfort as the conversation involved graphic language. As they talked, Hudson smoothly brought the conversation around to the matter at hand. Angela told them about her mother, Pamela Bivens, while her son played nearby with his pet ferret, legal to own in Nevada. The small, burrowing animal liked to climb into narrow places and the cuddly pet disappeared into some couch cushions.

She told Hudson that she and her mother had seen the news coverage about Thornton and Snyder being arrested in connection with the murder of the Las Vegas girl. Her mother, Angela said, then "told her a few things," that she hadn't shared before. Angela tried to get her mother to call police, but her mother was scared. Angela thought she might talk anonymously.

Hudson understood that Bivens was afraid of Thornton, so he agreed to speak with her anonymously. But did Angela know what Bivens wanted to tell them? Angela told them that her mother believed that her father was responsible for the disappearance of another young girl years before. Suddenly, Rushton gave a startled cry and doubled over. Hudson looked over to see why he would be so shocked at this news.

Rushton's face had turned bright red.

"The ferret ran up my pants leg," he said, as he tried to shake the little weasel out of his clothing.

Angela agreed to talk with her mother, and Hudson and Rushton spoke with her the next day. Bivens was clearly nervous about speaking with them. Like anyone who is anxious, she jumped around from subject to subject. Hudson let her talk for a while to see if that would calm her down. Bivens alternated between praising Thornton, as if to defend the fact that she had been married to him, and pointing out his flaws. She described her ex-husband as having an addictive personality: when he latched onto something, he would obsess over it. He was a chain smoker, and when he was introduced to methamphetamine, he progressively became addicted to it.

Thornton was a "pretty good bullshitter" who could turn on the charm, Bivens said, an asset in the beauty business. Surrounded by women, he was a funny, provocative, and flirtatious boss who infused the salons with a contagious energy. But he also had a darker side, a controlling side. He was particularly interested in the subject of mind control and manipulation. Bivens said that she often felt as if she had been brainwashed—her own words. Thornton had convinced her that she was fat and unattractive and that her own children didn't even like her.

Hudson wanted more than anything to find out what Bivens knew about the other missing girl, but he didn't want to risk pushing her, only to have her clam up. As she grew more comfortable talking with them, Hudson gently asked if she would describe her life with Thornton.

That's when the conversation turned to Janeen Snyder.

Rialto, California
March 1994

"Mom," Angela called as she walked in the front door, home from school. "Can my friend stay with us for a while?"

Pamela was forming the word "no" when she saw that her thirteen-year-old daughter had not brought her boyfriend home with her but a young girl.

"Hi," said the blond girl standing in front of her.

"This is my friend Janeen," Angela said, explaining that Janeen was her boyfriend's sister.

Pamela braced herself for her teenage daughter's idea of a logical argument. Angela was friends with Janeen Snyder, who was one year older than she. Angela had been dating Janeen's brother. She said that Janeen was having family trouble and didn't have a place to stay. Could she stay with them for a while? Bivens discussed it with her husband, and they talked to Janeen's mother about living arrangements. Janeen's mother agreed to pay the Thorntons twenty-five dollars a week to take care of Janeen during the time she was living with them, although she never paid. To her husband, Pamela had argued that Janeen needed a father and a mother figure but Thornton had made his decision once he laid eyes on Janeen. At thirteen, she had left childhood behind, skipped her awkward adolescent years, and was roaring into adulthood. Janeen was very aware of her sexual power, and it didn't go unnoticed by Thornton.

While watching TV after dinner one night, Thornton told Janeen everything a teenage girl yearned to hear. He told her that she was special and that he knew she was special because he had seen the northern lights in Alaska on the day she was born. He complimented her on her "cat eyes." Janeen was awed by this father figure, a powerful, successful businessman telling her that she was important to him. Shortly after Janeen moved her few bags of belongings into Angela's room, Angela broke up with Janeen's brother and started dating another boy, Allen Jiminez.

One month after Janeen moved in, Thornton rented a house in Lake Arrowhead on Matterhon Drive, which Pamela liked because it was "a status thing" to live in the ritzy resort town. They kept the Rialto house on Silver Circle Street so that the girls could continue to go to high school in Rialto instead of transferring to the high school in Lake Arrowhead. They lived at the Matterhorn Drive house for about a year, then the Thorntons moved into a home on lakefront property that had a dock on Lake Arrowhead. A part of the family now, Janeen accompanied the Thorntons during each of these moves, and participated in family vacations, holidays, and birthdays. Janeen's fourteenth birthday was celebrated with a Southern California childhood ritual, a pizza party at Chuck E.

Cheese, but after the party, Thornton gave Janeen a cupcake laced with drugs and sexually assaulted her. She ran away, but Thornton tracked her down a few months later. He continued to pursue her and kept telling her that she was special.

Months after moving to Lake Arrowhead, Janeen and Angela made a habit of cutting school and running back to Rialto to visit friends. Bivens once received a call from the Rialto Police Department informing her that Janeen and Angela had been arrested at Pic 'n Save, a discount department store, for shoplifting. Unfazed, Bivens picked up the two girls at the police station and brought them home to Lake Arrowhead.

Angela did not get along with her father, and Bivens said that during their arguments, Thornton would often turn violent. Bivens claimed that she was working full-time at the Perris hair salon and wasn't at home to stop it. After coming home from work one day, Bivens heard Thornton and Angela arguing, and then she heard him slapping her.

After that incident, Angela wanted to move out and Bivens reluctantly agreed. In retrospect, Bivens wondered how much of the tension between Angela and her father was linked to his interest in getting Angela out of the house to clear his access to Janeen. Angela was spending more time with her boyfriend, Allen Jimenez, than going to school, and at fifteen, she became pregnant. Thornton helped his daughter pack her things, and he drove her over to her boyfriend's house and dropped her off. Angela later married Jiminez, before moving with him and their son to Las Vegas.

Shortly after Angela left, Janeen moved in with a boyfriend in the Crestline area, but she stayed in touch. Thornton continued the strange back-and-forth relationship with Janeen. He would pick her up from wherever she was staying and bring her back home, even though she typically would leave again after a few days or a few weeks. Thornton kept telling her that they were destined to be together, and that she was his special partner. When Bivens and Thornton took family vacations, Janeen went with them. When Janeen turned sixteen, much to Bivens's chagrin, Thornton moved her back in with them. Thornton purchased another home in Lake Arrowhead, far up in the mountains, which would become Thornton and Snyder's retreat.

Bivens knew that her husband was obsessed with Janeen, but she thought that it would fade or he would grow tired of her, as he had of other obsessions. In nearly twenty years of marriage, Bivens had learned to look the other way, but Janeen wasn't going away and Thornton's obsession was growing. Though Thornton clearly was the dominant force, Janeen held considerable influence over him. By the time Bivens put her foot down, it was too late. Michael Jr. and Angela had already moved out, and Bivens wanted Thornton to herself again so they could enjoy their hard-earned affluence in their middle years. Janeen didn't fit into the plan. But Thornton leveraged the business to keep Bivens busy and at arm's length. He dropped out of the day-to-day operation of the salons, letting the daily burdens fall into her lap. Thornton told his wife that he had done the hard part by creating a successful empire. Why shouldn't he enjoy his life? How much trouble is it to just keep them running? Thornton said that he was now bored with the salons and wanted to do something else with his life. Bivens knew that "something else" involved Janeen Snyder, and she didn't understand why Thornton didn't just ask her for a divorce. But she waited, hoping that someday he would soon grow tired of Snyder, too, and come back to her.

Now at the helm of the salons, Bivens was consumed by the day-to-day operation of the beauty empire, and Thornton finally had the opportunity to ingratiate himself with Janeen. When Bivens objected to his spending so much time with her, Thornton paid lip service to his wife and moved Janeen out of the family home into a nearby apartment. Thornton again sexually assaulted the young teenager, telling her afterward that they were special. Both of them were different, he said. They were wolves, and other people were sheep. He told Janeen that wolves mated for life and he and Janeen were going to be partners for life. They would create a wolf pack that would prey on the sheep. It was their destiny, he said, to be soul mates.

Rialto, California
February 1996

Oh no, not again.

Cheryle Peters grabbed a pair of gloves and plucked the syringe out of the sink. One of the more popular stylists at the Fixx in San Dimas, Peters was an ex-heroin addict who had learned to style hair while serving a prison sentence at the California Institute for Women in Chino. She had fought hard to leave that lifestyle behind, straighten out her life, and raise her teenage daughter. The last thing she wanted was to be around drugs and around people who were still living that life. Not after what she'd been through. This was the third time in as many weeks that she had found a syringe in the salon. A month before that, Peters had found a fix kit—for injecting heroin—tucked neatly behind the cash register. The other stylists didn't know what it was, but Peters did. And she knew exactly to whom it belonged: Jill Raimondi, the new salon manager Michael Thornton had hired. An ex-con like Peters, she was still using. As a recovering heroin addict, Peters recognized the signs of addiction. She sometimes had to redo a client's hair to correct the mistakes Raimondi had made when she was high.

Seeing drug paraphernalia casually lying around the salon made the other hairstylists just as uncomfortable as Peters. Stylist Karla Corwin had also seen Raimondi's heroin kits and even saw her inject the drug and leave a mess in the sink for others to clean up. Like the other stylists, Corwin was too intimidated by Raimondi to complain, but Peters wasn't. She confronted her and was rebuffed, but then took her complaint to Thornton. To her astonishment, he told her to mind her own business.

Peters didn't like the fact that Thornton had chosen to look the other way. Both she and Corwin had noticed a change in Thornton and were suspicious about the way he'd been acting lately, waltzing into the salon at the close of the business day to open the cash register, scoop out the cash, and walk out without a word. They saw a young girl sitting in the front seat of his Suburban, and it wasn't his daughter. It wasn't any of Peters's business why he was tipping his own till, but if it had anything to do with why he tolerated a manager openly using drugs in his salon, she would have to leave. She was a single mother with problems of her own. Her fourteen-year-old daughter, Jessie, had hit the rebellious teenage years and Peters's lectures about staying in school and avoiding the path she had taken in life fell on deaf ears. How could Peters tell her daughter not to quit school, take drugs, run around with a bad crowd, and land in prison when that's exactly what she had done?

Perplexed, Peters talked with Corwin and the other stylists about what to do and Corwin said the problems reached beyond drug use. Corwin said that Raimondi was fixing the books and embezzling salon proceeds. Corwin was responsible for daily accounting at the salon, but Raimondi had instructed her to do the books in pencil each evening. The following day, Raimondi would change Corwin's accounting figures and re-write them in ink. Corwin and Peters checked the ledger and confirmed the alterations.

The other stylists thought they should just quit en masse, and another raised the idea of bypassing Thornton and filing a complaint with the state licensing board. Peters agreed that they should take action, but on one condition. Thornton had given her a chance to turn her life around, and she wanted to give him the same courtesy. When her daughter was having problems, Thornton had allowed Jessie to come to the salon a couple of times a week and stay the entire day, eight or nine hours. Peters thought that he was being kind when he once remarked that he found her daughter "beautiful." She wanted to try talking to Thornton one more time; this time, she would tell him that they had caught Raimondi embezzling money. She also thought it would be more convincing to tell him that if the state board learned about the heroin use at the salon, it could revoke his license and put theirs in jeopardy, too.

After their talk, Peters told Corwin and the other stylists that it seemed to work. Thornton had said that he would come out to the salon and "take care of the problem." Peters was happy; it was a challenge to find work with a prison record, and she didn't want to start looking again.

Sure enough, Thornton arrived a few days later and asked Peters and Corwin to talk to him alone. He escorted both stylists outside and they followed Thornton around the back of the building to the Dumpsters behind a supermarket, out of public view.

Peters and Corwin believed he intended to handle the matter civilly, but they quickly changed their minds when he started screaming at them to mind their own business. He told them not to tell anyone about Raimondi. Corwin told Thornton that police officers often came to the salon to get their hair cut and that none of the stylists wanted to go to jail because of Raimondi's drug problem. With that, Peters said Thornton "flipped out" and began attacking them verbally. They were so frightened as they rounded the corner and reentered the salon that they were shaking.

That was it. Thornton's irrational attack made their decision to quit that much easier. A third stylist joined them. The following morning, Corwin went to the salon at 5 a.m. to write down the names and contact information of her clients so that she could invite them to join her once she found a station at another salon.

All three stylists soon found work at a rival salon,

Split Ends. Corwin and the other stylist put the unsavory episode behind them, but Peters stuck to her principles and filed a complaint with the state board. She also filed for unemployment benefits for her part-time position. Since Peters hadn't been fired or laid off, she had to give justification for quitting in order to receive benefits. She reported that the Fixx maintained a hazardous work environment because of the drug-addicted manager.

The dispute at the shop upset Thornton, and he was even more upset to learn that Peters and Corwin had stood outside the Fixx salon, handing out flyers to direct customers to Split Ends. But what sent him over the edge was the complaint with the state Board of Cosmetology. It made him extremely angry, to the point where he became obsessed and couldn't let it go. At the hearing before a state administrative officer, Michael and Pamela Thornton portrayed themselves as kindly salon owners who had taken pity on Peters and given the recovering heroin addict a job because her status as a parolee was making it difficult for her to find work elsewhere. They said she had only filed a complaint so that she could stay at home and collect unemployment benefits. Peters was appalled, but she was relieved that the state claims officer gave Thornton's account no credence. She won the right for part-time benefits, but Thornton dug in his heels and filed an appeal. However, the prospect of an appeal wasn't enough to satisfy him. He was furious at Peters for putting his business in peril. He decided not to get mad, but to get even.

Didn't his ex-employee have a daughter?

**Glendora, California
March 29, 1996**

"Hi."

A scared and apprehensive Janeen Snyder knocked on the front door of the Peters residence and stood fidgeting on the front porch. Cheryle Peters answered the door and saw a petite girl with long, light brown hair and fine features, who was about her daughter's age. Janeen Snyder, sixteen at the time, was wearing a light-colored T-shirt and blue jeans and carried a backpack.

"Is that girl here?" Snyder asked in a small voice. Thornton had rehearsed with her, over and over, to prepare, but she appeared nervous and out of place.

"Why would you ask for my daughter and not even know her name?" Peters thought this was an odd request. Was this one of the teenagers Jessie was running around with? Was she selling something? Why wasn't she in school?

"I was sent to your door," Snyder said. "There's someone's waiting for me and, uh, your daughter around the corner." Snyder had never met Jessie, and Thornton could not remember her name.

"Who? Who's waiting?" Peters was about to slam the door in Snyder's face when Jessie, newly blond and in braces, stepped in between them and spoke to the girl on the doorstep. That was enough for Peters. She asked the girl to leave and she did. Peters closed the door and asked her daughter, "Who was that?"

"I don't know, Mom. Some girl," Jessie said.

Peters couldn't get a straight answer out of Jessie, and she had to get to work. Peters wasn't sure whether she believed her daughter, but she didn't blame her either. At Jessie's age, she was under a lot of pressure from her friends and was too young to understand that the restrictions imposed on her were for her own good. She wished that she could bring Jessie with her to the salon like she used to at the Fixx, but that wasn't allowed at Split Ends. Because of Jessie's problems at school, she was on a "home study" program, which meant that she had do her schoolwork from home. Peters sent Jessie back to her room to do her school work while Peters continued getting ready for work. She promised Jessie that she would call once she got to work. An hour or so later, Peters called from the salon and spoke with Jessie in the phony

British accents they had sometimes used when she was a little girl. They made plans like "proper ladies" for later that afternoon.

Around the corner from the Peters house, Janeen Snyder sat in the passenger seat of Thornton's car. He was red-faced and fuming.

"Go back there and do it," he screamed. Cheryle Peters had left for the salon, but they waited. Thornton prepared some methamphetamine for Snyder to pump her up before sending her back to knock on the front door.

"We are wolves," he said. "Other people are the sheep. You and I are special. We are a wolf pack.

"Now say it again like we practiced!" Thornton thundered.

"My uncle and I wanted to take you to the movies!" Snyder said, trying to appear relaxed and casual like they rehearsed. "He's waiting just around the corner. Let's go!"

Thornton sent her out again.

"This time," he told her, "don't come back without the girl."

Week after week, after long days of running the salons by herself, Pamela Thornton pulled into her driveway every night feeling emotionally and physically drained. Living in a constant state of fatigue allowed her little energy to deal with the overwhelming issues confronting her at home. Despite her husband's prolonged affair with Janeen, Pamela still loved him. Even though they had grown distant and Janeen had become entrenched in their lives, Pamela wondered if she was deluded to think that eventually everything would work out between the two of them and they could resume a normal life. Pamela couldn't get a grasp on how to fix it and found it more comfortable to remain in a state of denial. So when evidence turned up that her husband was draining the salons of cash to support his drug habit, she turned numb.

Pamela slowly sank into depression. She had no idea

how to stop her husband from philandering with a girl barely half his age, how to get him interested in their business again, or how to corral him back into the marital fold. She consulted a doctor to obtain a prescription for tranquilizers to dull her pain. Some days she felt so overwhelmed that it seemed too much trouble to get out of bed.

On March 29, she arrived home and had dinner with her husband and Janeen, as had become their routine. Thornton remarked that she looked tired and should go to bed. It was less a romantic invitation than a warning.

"Don't come out of your room. Even if you hear something, don't leave your room," he said.

Pamela took her usual regimen of pills and went to bed, but she found it hard to sleep. Throughout the night, she was awakened by odd thumping sounds from the bathroom. She heard noises, like something was being dropped and moved around. She also heard whispering. But she didn't leave her room.

The next morning, she overheard Thornton and Janeen talking.

"Did you see how long it took her to drown?" Thornton asked. Pamela was startled, but he wasn't talking to her.

"It took a long time," Snyder replied with a nod. They were talking about drowning a girl in the bathtub and cutting her up into pieces. Pamela heard her husband say Cheryle Peters's name but thought his talk about harming the ex-employee's daughter to get even with her was just that—talk.

"Won't her mother be surprised when her daughter doesn't come home?" Thornton said, chuckling. "She would probably think she just ran away and that she would never go home again."

As Pamela was leaving to go to work, she saw half a dozen new ice chests, ice, and concrete blocks scattered on the floor of the garage. Thornton and Snyder looked haggard, as though they had been up all night, and were talking about packing the last parts of a girl's body on ice in the ice chests. From what Pamela overheard, the ice would preserve the pieces until Thornton and Snyder could find a way to weigh them down and get rid of them. Thornton said they would load the ice chests into the boat and dump them in the ocean beyond Dana Point.

"What are we going to do with her—with it? With these?" Pamela heard Snyder say, gesturing toward the styrofoam ice chests. "I mean . . . how do we make it sink?"

"We have to wire the pieces to bricks," Thornton said, ". . . cinderblocks. That'll make 'em sink. We need to get wire."

Snyder made a face and lit a cigarette.

"You've got to attach them to something, otherwise they just float," Thornton said as if he was thinking aloud. "When the body deteriorates, it fills up with gases and it floats to the surface because air gets trapped inside. That's how you get caught—when they find a floating body. "

"We have to do something about the head; we have to attach it to something heavy," he said.

Snyder looked puzzled.

"How do you wire a cement block to a head?"

The following night, Thornton surprised Snyder with a present. He brought out a small, flat cardboard box illustrated with a Western theme and presented her with her own handgun. From now on, Thornton deemed it "mandatory" for Snyder to carry the gun when she was with him. She needed to be armed at all times. Over dinner, Thornton and Snyder celebrated the newest firearm and their status as a wolf pack.

Following the bizarre evening of odd noises, Pamela Thornton resumed her routine of running the salons single-handedly, coming home from work exhausted each night. She never looked too closely in the bathroom where all of the noises had come from that night to see if anything terrible had happened in there. She didn't usually use the bathroom in that part of the house and decided not to investigate. She also declined to look in the ice chests in the garage, nor did she ask her husband what was in them. She told herself that she didn't need to know.

Who was she to tell Michael what to do?

By this time, she had heard her husband talk about the stylist and the fact that her teenage daughter had been reported missing. From their conversations, she knew that their exchange had to do with the missing girl because Thornton had mentioned her by name. She was frightened and, even though she suspected that her own husband had done something terrible in her own house, she didn't want to go in there to look. Not only was she afraid at what she might find, she was afraid for her own life. She didn't want to know. She didn't want to get involved.

About three days later, Thornton and Snyder took the boat and all of the ice chests to Dana Point. This was unusual to Pamela because they usually boated on Lake Arrowhead. They had never taken the boat onto the ocean, although Pamela knew that her husband was familiar with Dana Point from deep sea fishing trips there.

Even though Pamela Thornton was a forty-year-old woman of considerable resources, she was too fearful to make an anonymous phone call to police. To admit that she was at home at the time a young girl was being drowned and dismembered in their bathtub wouldn't make her look like a very good person. Pamela knew the mother of the missing girl by name, since she was an ex-employee, but she never went to her. She didn't take any action that could come back to her and get Thornton angry. Thornton had told her that if she ever left him, he'd kill her. The conversations she had overheard between Thornton and Snyder about drowning, dismembering, then dumping a victim made Pamela think that she could be next.

Robert Presley Detention Center
December 2003

Each time Thornton wrote a page or two of his defense strategy letter, he would run it by Rea to see how it "sounded." Thus began their brainstorming sessions, as Thornton called them. He would spell out exactly what happened in the days leading up to Michelle's murder. Then Thornton would bounce ideas off Rea to get a feel for what "truth" felt right for the letter. Based on Rea's input, Thornton would make changes in the letter.

Thornton had one more favor to ask. He wanted Rea to take his handwritten pages and transcribe them in his own, much neater printing to prevent a forensic handwriting analyst from linking the letter to Thornton, who didn't want to be caught manipulating the facts of their story. Then, once Rea was released, he would deliver the letter to Snyder's attorney.

Rea agreed, at first. But the more he thought about it, he realized that he had just raised his profile from being an anonymous messenger to becoming the sole person who could be forensically linked to the document. He was uncomfortable with the way Thornton pushed the boundaries of his willingness to help him. If Thornton didn't want to be associated with his own letter, Rea wondered, why would Rea write the letter in his handwriting and be left holding the bag, so to speak? A few days later, Rea suggested that instead of writing the letter he would type it up before he delivered it. To his relief, Thornton agreed. Now Rea simply collected Thornton's handwritten pages. Every time Thornton finished a page, he gave it to Rea to keep to prevent deputies from finding it during regular searches of Thornton's cell.

The letter gradually took shape as the pair walked circles in the day room for exercise, with Rea serving as Thornton's muse, messenger, and sounding board for his theories. Each day, he offered tidbits of insight to Rea about his unusual relationship with Snyder. Thornton explained that people who survive a traumatic experience with others, like a natural disaster, generate intense emotions that result in a powerful bond. Thornton hinted to Rea that he had exploited that tendency in Snyder by subjecting her to trauma to evoke the bonding response. Thornton was smiling as he talked as if he was describing something pleasant and fun, and Rea fought to maintain a constant facial expression. He wondered if he had misunderstood Thornton: what kind of trauma was he talking about?

Rea felt increasingly guilty about helping Thornton and wondered if he was committing a crime by doing so. He paid closer attention to Thornton without letting him know that he was getting suspicious about their project and the tenor of his relationship with Snyder. The more time went by, the more Thornton shared with Rea, as long as no other inmates were near enough to overhear. The details Thornton shared created tension for Rea, and he found it challenging to suppress his reactions. He had to train himself not to register stress in his facial expressions and to only show Thornton interest or curiosity so that he would continue talking. Rea stayed quiet and never asked Thornton questions. Thornton continued sharing his letters from Snyder, but Rea got the sense that he really didn't love her as much as he told her that he did. Thornton bragged that from the time he met Snyder as a young teenager, he had deliberately manipulated her emotions. He had molded her. He read extensively about psychological experiments and tested his theories on her. Rea realized that Snyder was not the love of Thornton's life as he had claimed. Rea wondered: Did Thornton have something in store for Snyder other than shielding her from a murder rap?

Days later, he got the answer. Thornton told Rea that the prosecution's forensic tests showed that Snyder, not he, had gunshot residue on her hands. This meant that Thornton could blame Snyder for the shooting. According to his reasoning, he could be held responsible for a lesser charge or penalty because she was the shooter (although that is not the law as it pertains to the facts of this case). Rea finally confirmed that Thornton didn't care for Snyder the way that he initially talked about her. Thornton was using her and thought he could get away with it.

If that was the case, Rea didn't want to be manipulated by Thornton either. That got him thinking: What would happen if he turned the tables on Thornton? He had to think it through. He had never shared with Thornton why he was in protective custody. He ran the risk of having the circumstances of his confinement made known, but that would be the least of his worries if he became a snitch. Behind jail walls, an unprotected inmate who testifies against another inmate can be subjected to the worst possible abuse, at the least, and deadly violence, at the worst.

To play this dangerous game, Rea had to be smart. There's only so much that jail authorities can do to protect an inmate, and the one person who was beginning to terrify him the most was living in the cell next to his.

This photo depicting Michael Thornton and Janeen Snyder with legs intertwined on the couch showed law enforcement that underlying the couple's violent acts was a committed romantic relationship. *Exhibit from criminal trial*

The primary Thornton family home in Rialto had fallen into disrepair and the grass overgrown after being used as a meth den. *Courtesy of Riverside County Sheriff's Department*

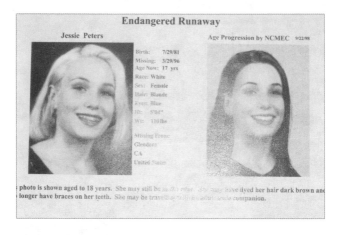

Endangered Runaway

Jessie Peters

Age Progression by NCMEC   9/22/98

Birth: 7/29/81
Missing: 3/29/96
Age Now: 17 yrs
Race: White
Sex: Female
Hair: Blonde
Eyes: Blue
Ht: 5'04"
Wt: 110 lbs

Missing From:
Glendora
CA
United States

photo is shown aged to 18 years. She may still be in this area. She may have dyed her hair dark brown and longer have braces on her teeth. She may be traveling with an adult male companion.

Cheryle Peters longed to find her daughter years after her disappearance, coordinating with local police and a national missing child agency to create a poster showing what Jessie would have looked like three years after Thornton and Snyder kidnapped and killed her.

Exhibit from criminal trial

Snyder's grisly pencil sketch depicts the dismemberment of a body, the bleeding pieces weighed down by cinder blocks in the same way Jessie Peters was murdered.

Exhibit from criminal trial

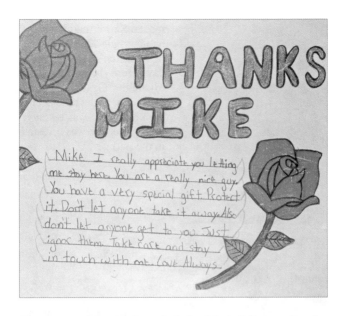

Thornton and Snyder forced victim Maria Rivera to list the benefits of staying with them, such as being treated with respect, with the idea that her letter would prove that she was happy to stay with them.

Exhibit from criminal trial

Thornton was arrested and handcuffed in the backyard of a home in the Loring Ranch development after fleeing the tack room of the Lindholm Ranch after Michelle Curran was killed. He was still wet from hosing blood from his hands and clothing.

Exhibit from criminal trial

Janeen Snyder had just had her hair done by one of Thornton's stylists the day before she murdered Michelle Curran in the tack room at the ranch. The booking photo was taken hours after she was arrested in the park.

Exhibit from criminal trial

Teams of detectives and forensic techs searched the VW and the horse trailer outside the tack room in a vain attempt to find a severely injured or deceased person.

Exhibit from criminal trial

When Diane Lindholm opened the door to the trailer, she found the body of Michelle Curran curled up in a small saddle compartment. *Courtesy of Riverside County Sheriff's Department*

Thornton snapped this instant photo of Michelle, wearing the Independent shirt she had on when she was kidnapped, and a stone-faced Snyder in the front seat of the Suburban. *Exhibit from criminal trial*

The detectives who converged on Thornton and Snyder's Running Springs cabin after their arrest found the walls decorated with violent images, photos of wolves and a white, plush teddy bear hung in a noose.

Courtesy of Riverside County Sheriff's Department

Detective George Hudson and the other detectives who searched the Running Springs cabin were interested to find Snyder's collage art adorning the walls with the words "killer," "shooting strangers," and "big bucks" smeared with red paint to look like blood.

Exhibit from criminal trial

During the detectives' search of the Running Springs cabin, Detective Steve Welch found a tunnel under the tread of the stairs to a secret room dug into the hillside.

Exhibit from criminal trial

While confined and awaiting trial, Thornton and Snyder used the mail service from jail to send coded messages. Snyder adorned the letters and envelopes with romance-themed artwork, which Deputy District Attorney Michael Rushton used to disprove Snyder's attorney's argument that she had been manipulated by Thornton, not a willing, romantic partner.

Exhibit from criminal trial

The Curran family created a memorial to Michelle in their Las Vegas home, which included the wall-sized poster made by her high school friends and her favorite Dalmation stuffed animals.

Exhibit from criminal trial

Five

On the forty-five minute drive to Cheryle Peters's house, Hudson reviewed with Rushton their strategy for dealing with a sensitive witness. Now was not the time to break the news that her daughter was dead. To be fair, they didn't have independent confirmation that it was, in fact, Jessie Peters who drowned in the bathtub that night or that anyone had actually been killed. In legal terms, they had a strong suspicion, but no proof.

A week had passed since Hudson had learned from Bivens about the strange noises she had heard that night. During that week, he had tracked down former salon manager Jill Raimondi at the Cedar House Rehabilitation Center, a halfway house and drug treatment center in the Riverside area, the same kind of transitional living facility where Raimondi and Peters had first been taught hair styling so that they could earn a living after their release. Raimondi acknowledged to Hudson that she had been using heroin and embezzling salon proceeds to fund her habit at that time. She didn't remember the name of the stylist who had confronted her but gave Hudson the name of another stylist who had worked there at the same time, Karla Corwin. Hudson tracked down Corwin, and he and Rushton interviewed her a few hours later at her home in Diamond Bar. Corwin gave them Cheryle Peters's name. She remembered that Peters's daughter had disappeared shortly after the dispute with Thornton.

"We'll work the angle that she has a missing daughter," Hudson said on the way to the Peters residence. "We'll just follow it up as a missing persons case and tell her that we may have some information and see what she what she has to say."

The most thoughtful approach with Peters, Hudson said, would be to get her to independently verify what Bivens had told them, and then, after doing the necessary investigative homework to confirm Bivens's account, they could tactfully give Peters the proper death notification regarding her daughter.

Rushton agreed.

Hudson hadn't wanted to have this kind of discussion with a prosecutor, but in the few days he had worked with Rushton, he had been frustrated with his habit of interrupting witness interviews. Most prosecutors that he'd worked with over the years would simply let him do his job. Hudson hoped that Rushton would back off after the publicity had died down.

Hudson pulled into a mobile home park in Glendora, one of dozens of bedroom communities surrounding Los Angeles, and found Cheryle Peters's home. It was noticeably smaller than the double-wide and single-wide trailers surrounding it, instead resembling an RV one would use for a vacation. As they got out of the car, Rushton hesitated. Hudson walked up to the door and knocked. It was a cold call: Cheryle Peters had no idea they were coming. When she opened the door, Hudson showed her his police badge and explained that they wanted to speak with her about her missing daughter. She kindly invited them in, but Rushton suddenly interjected and suggested instead that they go to a nearby coffee shop. Peters hesitated, and Hudson shot Rushton a glance. It was a very warm day, and the trailer was hot, small, and looked well lived-in. He knew that Rushton was a perfectionist who drove an immaculate car and had a standing appointment every week to get his hair cut. Rushton once told Hudson that he had even dug up flowers his wife had planted because he thought they were in the wrong spot in the yard. Hudson figured that Rushton didn't want to sit in a hot, tiny trailer because of his predilection for cleanliness and detail, character quirks that may have made him a successful prosecutor, but to the outsider would seem insensitive, particularly to a woman whose daughter had probably been viciously murdered by these people. Although she would feel more comfortable in her own home, Hudson suggested a compromise—they could talk in the air-conditioned car. To his chagrin, Rushton held out for the coffee shop. Unwilling to argue in front of Peters, Hudson went along.

On the way, Peters excitedly peppered them with questions. What did they know about her daughter? Had they found her? Did they have any leads? She thought Jessie was a runaway, and it was obvious that she was desperate for any scrap of evidence that her daughter was alive. Over the years, friends had passed along sightings of young women resembling Jessie at a mall, a gas station, and waiting for a bus. Peters's family had suffered a painful split after Jessie's disappearance; one faction of the family believed that Peters's former life as a drug addict had a role in the girl's disappearance. Peters dreamed of seeing Jessie again some day and healing the chasm in her family.

To Hudson's dismay, no sooner had they sat down in the coffee shop when Rushton broke the terrible news.

"We've arrested two people, and we think they may have killed your daughter," Rushton blurted.

As soon as the words left Rushton's lips, the horrified woman let out an uncontrolled wail. Thunderstruck, she sobbed with deep anguish. Out came years of pent-up grief, the finality of knowing that her daughter had been murdered. She would never mend fences with her family, never see her daughter get married, and never see her grandchildren. Both men sat in silence waiting for the emotions to subside, but Peters's sobs grew louder.

Hudson fumed. This was exactly what he had wanted to avoid. The poor woman had probably not had a good night's sleep for five years, Hudson thought, and they had taken her out of her own home to give her heartbreaking news in a public place because this deputy district attorney didn't want to sit in her humble trailer. Hudson thought that this was unnecessary, if not unkind, to this witness and it didn't further their investigation. Peters was causing such a scene at the coffee shop that the two men drew stares from the other customers. Hudson tried his best to calm her down, but as an investigator, he had to maintain a professional distance. It was obvious that Peters was too distraught for them to conduct the interview, so they drove her home. She agreed to meet with them the next day at the Glendora Police Department.

On the drive back to the office, Hudson held his tongue; he had nothing to say. When he had been assigned this case, Hudson and Rushton had discussed their strategy for preparing the case for trial, as would any colleagues working on the same team with a common goal. The investigator's job is to find new facts, new evidence, new witnesses, and old witnesses, and track additional crimes in addition to bolstering the current case. They conduct interviews and sometimes the deputy district attorney goes along. But Hudson felt that Rushton had started taking over the interviews in Las Vegas. He asked one question, then another and another. Soon, Rushton dominated the interview, reducing Hudson's role to note-taker. Hudson hated that. He had heard other investigators complain about Rushton's propensity for taking over interviews and had tried to head it off when they talked for the first time, and that seemed to have been as effective as their talk before the interview with Peters. Hudson knew that nothing would be solved that night, so he focused on his mental checklist.

The case seemed to be exploding in a hundred directions at once, but Hudson was not easily flustered. Multiple searches had yielded too many items for forensics to catalogue. The tan Suburban, the Running Springs cabin, the Lake Arrowhead home, and a van parked near it were packed with the defendants' personal belongings, including a lot of guns, a couple of rifles and ammunition of all varieties, including hollowpoint bullets. And there was still another home to search, the Mesa, Arizona, home of Jean Evans, Michael Thornton's mother. Thornton's sister, Ricky Jo Cartwright, had heard of her brother's arrest and suggested to Detective Robert Joseph that investigators collect a few boxes of personal belongings and a green Jeep Wrangler Sport from their mother's house. Detective Joseph contacted the Maricopa County Sheriff's Department, which sent deputies on April 29 to Evans' home at Leisure World, a senior citizen's community just outside Phoenix. This didn't require a warrant, since the deputies were acting at the behest of the property owners and picked up only what Cartwright had specified. The officers filled three patrol cars with boxes of Thornton's personal effects and then sealed up the Jeep for transport to a police impound lot. Everything, including the vehicle, would eventually be transported to Riverside. While Hudson and Rushton had been conducting interviews with Angela Thornton and Pamela Bivens, Riverside investigators had been obtaining search warrants to conduct a search of Evans' home and, because of a legal technicality, to search the interior of the Jeep that had been collected. During the search of Evans' home, the detectives seized bedding and bedspreads, boxes of tools, a Gateway computer, several boxes of various types of ammunition, a box for a Ruger 9 mm handgun, a scrapbook titled "Partners" with vacation photos, and documents related to Thornton's stint in the Air Force. They also found a fat file of legal documents pertaining to a court case Thornton and Snyder had been involved with less than a year before their arrest, as well as a checkbook with Michael Thornton's name on it bearing his mother's Leisure World address.

Now that detectives had boxes upon boxes of evidence from the searches of Thornton's multiple homes and vehicles, it still was too early in the investigation to poinpoint which pieces of evidence would become relevant to their case, particularly since the case had doubled within the space of a week with the discovery that Thornton and Snyder may have been responsible for the murder of Jessie Peters. It would take weeks, if not months, to sort through everything before choosing particular items for examination by the sheriff's department's forensics laboratory. One item of evidence that came to Detective Joseph's attention was the padlock on the gate to Lindholm's property. He had compared it to the padlock that had been in Thornton's pocket when he was arrested. A key from Diane Lindholm had opened both of the padlocks. Lindholm had identified the padlock taken from Thornton's pocket as the missing padlock from the tack room door, leaving no doubt that he and Snyder were responsible for what had happened there.

By the time Hudson spoke with Diane Lindholm, the trauma she had suffered from the break-in had been compounded by the gruesome experience of finding a murder victim. Even though Lindholm had spoken with several detectives over the course of just one week, Hudson, a lifelong horse enthusiast who rode his horse as often as he could, quickly found common ground with her. She told him that her dogs had not acted normally since the break-in, and that she had seen one of them carrying around a pair of glasses. That explained why some evidence had appeared to be missing during the various searches by detectives. Hudson made a mental note to tell

Detectives Angeli, Knudson, and Welch that the unseen perpetrators who had been moving evidence around the crime scene had been four-legged.

When Hudson returned from Las Vegas and Arizona, he saw the results of the autopsy on Michelle Curran. Because her remains had lain deteriorating for five days, nearly drained of blood, there was an insufficient amount of blood to test, but a preliminary test on Michelle's urine revealed "significant" quantities of methamphetamine and marijuana. The cause of death, a single gunshot to the head, was no surprise, but the body revealed other, more gruesome details. Michelle had been sexually assaulted. She had suffered multiples scrapes and bruises from being struck repeatedly in addition to blunt force trauma to her mouth from being socked hard enough to draw blood and leave a bruise. The coroner confirmed that her wrists and ankles first had been bound with duct tape, which then was removed and replaced with plastic cable ties around each wrist and ankle and secondary zip ties interlaced with each of the four primary ties. This would have allowed immobilization of her arms and legs by securing them to a secondary object. The coroner found pressure marks from the multiple ligatures on her ankles, indicating that her feet and ankles had been stretched or pulled away from her body and that the marks on her body seemed to have been caused by using the ligatures to suspend her. The thin, tight plastic ties had cut more deeply into the back of her ankles than into the front, and there were similarly uneven marks around her wrists. The coroner concluded, as Detectives Angeli had suspected and Hudson had feared, that the tack had been configured to interlock with the zip ties around the victim's arms and legs to hang her by her ankles and wrists.

The coroner concluded that the force could have been applied by hanging the victim upside down, allowing her captors to ratchet the combination of tack and ligatures to stretch and suspend her from her four extremities in any fashion. She might have been suspended between

the wall and the center beam of the tack room, or simply
hung upside down against the wall. The reason for sus-
pending the victim wasn't simply for the purpose of sexual assault, when Thornton and Snyder had a furnished
motel room awaiting them, nor was it to prevent escape,
when mere duct tape and the presence of multiple guns
would suffice. If they had simply wanted to kill her, then
there was no need to remove her clothes, invade another's property, and go through the trouble of rearranging
the tack.

The bullet wound to the victim's head created stip-
pling, a peppering of gunshot residue on her skin, indicating that the shooter had held the gun no more than
twenty-four inches from her face when the fatal shot was
fired. The gunshot was "perfect," in the sense that it was
nearly in dead center of her forehead and completed a nearly
flawless straight trajectory from the front to the back of her
head, meaning the victim was absolutely still when the
shot was fired.

Hudson knew that a defendant's actions inform the
criminal charges that are filed, and in this case the charges
were mounting. In addition to murder, Thornton and Snyder would face charges of kidnapping, sexual assault,
and, with the details about the tack room, torture.

To Hudson, the most excruciating detail of the coroner's report was the victim's size. At five feet, two inches
tall, Michelle Curran weighed just eighty-one pounds.

Based on the motel receipts found in the Suburban,
Detectives Joseph had sent investigators to follow the
trail of motels and issue search warrants for the bank records connected to the credit cards used for the motel
stays. He even had investigators track down and interview clerks who had checked in Thornton and Snyder at
each of the motels.

It was too early in the investigation to start shipping
items of evidence to forensics for comparison and examination, particularly since Hudson had uncovered the pos-

sibility that the couple had committed a second homicide. Other bits and pieces of information were coming from Pamela Bivens, including another overheard conversation between Thornton and Snyder, who were bragging about killing two hitchhikers and mutilating their bodies. Bivens also mentioned a murder-for-hire in Tulsa, Oklahoma, for which Thornton had been paid $5,000 in cash and a car. Despite these shocking admissions, Hudson suspected from the way Bivens answered their questions that she still wasn't telling him everything she knew. Hudson didn't know whether Bivens was afraid of Thornton and Snyder, or whether she was worried that she could be held accountable for knowledge of criminal acts.

As a former sheriff's deputy, major crimes investigator detective, and a longtime investigator for the district attorney's office, Hudson had been around long enough to suspect that he was barely scratching the surface of the horrific acts the defendants had committed. What else they had done? Hudson thought it would be a good idea to have a long talk with Pamela Bivens about this purported murder in Tulsa.

Tulsa, Oklahoma
October 23, 1996, 5:50 A.M.

The GMC Sonoma pickup truck broke the stillness of daybreak as it roared through the residential outskirts of Tulsa. Thornton, in the passenger seat, directed Snyder to slow down and dim the headlights as they pulled up and parked across the street from their target location. The small, beige, single-frame house bordered by a chain-link fence sat at the bend in the road, where Park View Street dead-ended into Oak Street, the two streets forming an L shape. The modest homes had small yards, but the flat, empty horizon beckoned far beyond the neighborhood. Thornton had donned a construction hard hat over a blond wig with a ponytail hanging down the back, plastic glasses, and brown coveralls zipped to his mid-chest. He held a loaded, .38-caliber Taurus revolver in his lap. As they waited in the truck, Snyder fumbled in the semi-darkness preparing Thornton a line of methamphetamine—for "afterward."

After a few minutes, Sylvia Springer emerged from a house across the street with her three-year-old son, Jesse, in her arms and holding her six-year-old daughter, Donna Jo, by the hand. It was a chilly, fall morning, and the children were bundled up for the cold. The woman opened the door to a brown, older model Cutlass Supreme, flipped back the driver's seat and began strapping the toddler into the child seat.

"Hello, Ma'am!" Thornton walked across the street and approached the woman in her driveway. The gun was in his right front jacket pocket. He was holding a metal clipboard as if he were a utility serviceman.

"Yes?" Sylvia Springer did not recognize Thornton, but she noticed that he was wearing an odd-looking wig under a cap.

"Are you Miss Sylvia Springer?" Thornton asked.

"Yes," she answered. "What is this about?" Springer and her husband were separated after both had been arrested for drug possession. Though he was serving a prison sentence, she had successfully completed rehab and had turned her life around. In the meantime, she was battling her mother-in-law, Ricky Jo Cartwright, for custody of her children. She was headed to court that morning for the final hearing to gain custody from Cartwright.

"Did you report a gas leak?" Thornton asked.

As the man came closer, Springer noticed that he had dark hair underneath the wig and he had bloodshot eyes behind thick, dark-rimmed glasses. His jacket was zipped to the mid-chest.

"No," Springer said. "Maybe someone else did." Her toddler was already strapped into the backseat of the car and Donna Jo had already climbed into the front seat. They were ready to go.

Then she saw the gun in his hand.

"What do you want? What are you doing with that gun?" Springer stammered. She turned to Donna Jo and told her to run inside the house, then turned back to the man. The man didn't ask her for money; she wondered what he did want.

Then he started shooting.

The first bullet struck Springer in the left shoulder, and she screamed as she tried to run. Thornton continued shooting as she fell to the ground screaming. As the mother of two lay writhing in the driveway, Thornton kept firing. The next bullet hit her left thigh, and another entered her right forearm and emerged on the other side. Then Thornton aimed for her head and fired.

Springer lay dazed and bleeding in her driveway, feeling a sense of lost time. Somehow, she saw the man walk across the street, get into the truck, and drive away. Donna Jo watched the car drive away, then turn around and pass the house again. The man who had just gunned down her mother still had his passenger-side door open. He whistled a low tone like a bird and said softly, "Good-bye."

With the help of her brave little girl, Springer crawled back toward her house and their frightened cries awakened Springer's boyfriend, who called 9-1-1. She was transported to the hospital and into surgery. Surgeons removed the bullets from her shoulder and forearm, but they could not remove the bullet from her right temple. The fourth bullet in her left inner thigh was too close to an artery to remove.

Despite the four gunshot wounds at close range, Springer's doctors gave her a positive prognosis for recovery, though custody of her two children was temporarily awarded to her mother-in-law. When she was able to speak with investigators, Springer said that she didn't think the shooting was random because the man dressed as a utility serviceman seemed to walk straight toward her. She said that visitors often head to the wrong street, since her house faces the other side of the L-shaped street.

After the shooting, Thornton snorted the line of methamphetamine that Snyder had laid out for him, which gave him a quick, intense high, then demanded that Snyder perform a sexual act on him after they drove away.

"Did you see the way her head flew back when I shot her?" Thornton bragged.

Thornton and Snyder had borrowed Pamela's 1991 black GMC truck to drive out to Oklahoma for a two-week road trip to visit Thornton's older sister, and Springer's mother-in-law, Ricky Jo Cartwright. Pamela stayed behind to run the business but would fly out a couple of weeks later to join them at Cartwright's home in Tulsa, Oklahoma.

In September, Thornton had purchased a gun for Pamela at A1 Wholesale Guns on Foothill Boulevard in Rialto, near one of their homes. Thornton chose a .380 Taurus five-shot, double-action revolver, and registered it to Pamela. He picked up the gun after the mandatory fifteen-day waiting period and took it with him on the trip to Tulsa.

Bivens later told investigators that in his preparation for the trip to Oklahoma, Thornton spoke frequently with his sister, more than he usually did, but that didn't seem unusual since they were going to visit her. Bivens had considered the Tulsa trip a Thornton family affair. She and her mother-in-law, Jean Evans, flew to Oklahoma and met Thornton and Snyder at Cartwright's house. Thornton had given Pamela explicit instructions, if she arrived in Tulsa before he and Snyder did, to collect an envelope from his mother. Pamela did arrive before them, and her mother-in-law handed her a thick envelope that looked and felt like it was stuffed with cash. When Thornton arrived, she turned the envelope over to her husband. When he opened it, she saw a stack of bills that she estimated to be $5,000. The family visit was even more special because Cartwright's two young grandchildren were staying with her while their mother recuperated in the hospital from being shot in her driveway during an early-morning attack. To Pamela's surprise, Cartwright gave Thornton an unexpected gift, a 1987 Dodge Xplorer van that had been converted to a camper. After the visit, Pamela, Evans, and Cartwright drove the camper-van to Evans's home in Mesa, Arizona, where Pamela eventually caught a flight home. Thornton and Snyder drove back in Pamela's GMC truck.

When they reunited at their home in Lake Arrowhead, Pamela overheard conversations between Thornton and Snyder about what had occurred in Oklahoma.

"Did you see how much blood there was?" Thornton said. "Did you see how it splattered when I shot her?"

It sounded to Pamela like Thornton was bragging.

"Yeah," Snyder said. "The blood was going everywhere."

"I had to have killed her," Thornton said. "There was no way those wounds weren't fatal. I can't believe she didn't die."

"Uh-huh," Snyder said.

Thornton laughed at news reports that he had been wearing a Davy Crockett hat.

"How can a blond wig and a hard hat be confused with a Davy Crockett hat?" Thornton said.

As it turned out, the little girl, who was described by police as a very certain and calm witness, had said the shooter was an older white male, five feet, ten inches tall, 180 pounds, with gray hair under a hard hat with a tail hanging down the back, similar to a coonskin cap. It was the news media that had been confused, not the pint-sized witness.

After the trip to Oklahoma, Thornton bought matching black trenchcoats for Snyder and himself, bragged to their friends that they were "hit men," and even offered up

their services. The couple had arrived in Tulsa early
enough to pick up the Sunday newspaper before the attack on Springer. When they got home, Snyder memori-
alized the shooting with a collage made with Tulsa
newspaper clippings and pinned her artwork to the cabin
wall. Using headlines from major sections of the Sunday
paper, she arranged BUSINESS next to MONEY, then wrote
"NO" next to LIVING, and added "MORE PAIN. NOW WE'RE
EVEN." The entire piece reads: "BUSINESS. MONEY. NO
LIVING. MORE PAIN. NOW WE'RE EVEN." This indicated to
law enforcement that their business in Tulsa was for
money, the result of which was "no living." The shooting
of Springer represented payback to Cartwright, who
regained custody of her grandchildren. Despite efforts of
police in Tulsa to identify the culprits responsible for the
early morning shooting, the investigation yielded little
beyond the eyewitness account from the traumatized
youngster, and neither Ricky Jo, Thornton, his mother,
nor anyone else was ever prosecuted by authorities there.

Conveniently for law enforcement years later, Snyder
chose clips that clearly showed the month and year of
their trip. It was one of her first works of art to memorial-
ize their violent exploits. Later, she would adorn their
walls with other artwork, including photographs of snarl-
ing wolves, Thornton's gift of a Certificate of Homicide,
and more of her unique collages that paid homage to
murder.

Thornton rented a videotape of the movie *Natural
Born Killers* and told Snyder to watch it as her training
video. Restless at seventeen, Snyder alternated between
staying with the Thorntons, living with her mother, and
visiting friends. Snyder faced increasing hostility from
Pamela, who vacillated between trying to save her twenty-
four-year marriage to Thornton and wanting to walk
away from him, their homes, and the business she helped
build. Snyder loved the power and freedom she had with
Thornton and fell easily into the carefree braggadocio

and casual violence. But a remnant of Snyder's fractured childhood psyche emerged, and terrified of the two bloody attacks in six months, she did the only thing a frightened child has the power to do.

She ran away.

Six

Lake Arrowhead, California
March 1994

To the nearly fifty stylists at the Fixx chain of salons, Michael Thornton was a charming, flirtatious boss who was always quick with a quip or a compliment. When he wasn't doing paperwork from a back office in the Rialto salon, he made the rounds of each store, delivering bon mots with clean towels and supplies. To neighbors, the Thorntons were flush with the trappings of an intact, upwardly mobile family with posh, pine-bedecked second and third vacation homes in status-conscious Lake Arrowhead. But the cars, the homes, the boat, and the annual income that topped $1 million masked the darkness rooted in the Thorntons' family life. To Pamela and Angela, Thornton was their abuser. His wife and daughter helped Hudson peel away the veneer of the happy family and expose the decay at its center—a middle-aged man possessed by addiction, obsession, and abuse. When Thornton was focused and busy, he was happy and the abuse either vanished or significantly decreased. When he was unhappy, stressed, or under pressure, he exploded verbally and physically against his wife and children.

Pamela knew that she had no real control over her husband's violent temper, but she tried to mitigate it by keeping him occupied. One of the triggers for Thornton's violent temper was Michael Jr.'s struggle with a learning disability. His poor schoolwork served as a source of disappointment for Thornton. Instead of seeking educational assistance or a tutor to help his son, Thornton vented his rage with verbal and physical abuse. He had struck Pamela too many times to count and even tried to burn her with a cigarette, but what frightened her most was when Thornton raised his fists to the children. He kicked a sleeping Angela for eating his ice cream and struck her in the mouth when she was a young teenager still wearing metal orthodontia. When Michael Jr. turned eighteen, Thornton kicked him out of the house. That narrowed the targets of his rage to Pamela and Angela.

Hoping to quell the violence, Pamela fed her husband ideas for projects, being cautious about dropping suggestions so that the ideas would appear to come from him. Sometimes the process of shopping for another car or planning a vacation sufficiently consumed him, though his internal demons were never far behind. When he tired of a project, she would give him something else to chew on—like looking for another house to buy and weighing the pros and cons of moving to Lake Arrowhead. But just months before they moved, Thornton got his first taste of methamphetamine when he and Pamela were having dinner with some friends. The friends had purchased the drug in order to sell it and make money, but they wanted to "test" it first. That night in the early spring of 1994 was the first time that Pamela saw her husband use the drug, and he liked it. He liked it a lot. Pamela noticed that he dropped in on those friends more frequently, but his appetite for the drug was tempered by the consuming nature of everyday business operation, not to mention their plan to move to Lake Arrowhead.

Thornton loved the mountains, Pamela told Hudson. Both of them did. The air was fresh and clean, and it was peaceful. The change of seasons was different from the climate of the Inland Empire, which ranged from warm and smoggy to unbearably hot and smoggy. Because Thornton felt relaxed and happy there, the mountains also appealed to Pamela and she also thought the natural surroundings would help Angela. After years of abuse, Angela was careening into adolescence with unruly behavior, and Pamela thought that the move to Lake Arrowhead would have a calming effect on the entire family. Thornton found a house as picturesque as the street name suggested—Matterhorn Drive—and leased it for a year while he scouted for something permanent. Snyder joined the household one month before the move, and Pamela saw that taking her in had provided her husband with another distraction. In 1994, the Thorntons moved into the house on Matterhorn Drive as a family—Pamela, Michael, Angela, and Janeen.

Pamela isn't certain which of her husband's newfound obsessions created such a drastic change in him after the move—the methamphetamine, Janeen, or the remote mountain area—but after their first year, Pamela noticed clear signs of his addiction in her husband. He stayed up all day and night to work on the computer for two to three days in a row. He lost weight, smoked cigarettes incessantly, and acquired a nervous tic, an odd slurping noise with his mouth. The more time Thornton spent in the mountains, the less he liked going "down the hill" into the city and simply lost all interest in the business they had created. She told herself that her husband needed a break after working hard for so many years. Pamela realized as she got up every day and went down the hill to run the businesses that she was leaving a teenager who had been entrusted to their care with a middle-aged man who was quickly becoming addicted to meth. Despite the physical abuse, the questionable relationship with Snyder, and

Thornton's meth habit, Pamela thought that everything was fixable. She was still in love with her husband and hoped one day to recapture the man she had married and return to the life they once had.

Pamela believed that her husband would grow tired of the girl and the drugs, or that Snyder would leave him for someone her own age. And she did leave from time to time, but Thornton would find her and bring her back. In November 1996, she left again, and this time her birth mother filed a missing juvenile report, even though she rarely saw her daughter anyway. Snyder's latest departure coincided with Angela's return to the cabin. She had broken her leg and moved temporarily into the Blue Jay cabin with her husband while she recuperated. In her father's household once again, Angela boldly told her father to stop beating her mother, but he brushed her off. After a particularly bad fight, Angela pleaded with her mother to leave and offered to call police. She offered to help her mother find a place to live, but Pamela didn't want to go. She didn't believe in divorce.

Numbed by prescription drugs for anxiety, depression, and insomnia, Pamela remained in deep denial about her husband's behavior and his disturbing boasts about committing murder, and Snyder's absence reinforced her belief that their life eventually would return to normal again—once her husband got past his mid-life crisis.

Robert Presley Detention Center
Riverside, California
December 2003

If you can train rats, Thornton believed, you can train a teenager.

Rea never paid much attention to Thornton's ramblings about women . . . but rat training? In the laboratory experiment, rats were placed on a metal sheet and received a small shock when music played, he told Rea during one of their walks around the day room. It was similar to the game of musical chairs, only in reverse. When the rats learned to remain motionless at hearing the music, they no longer received a shock and thus were no longer afraid of music. Thornton told Rea that he applied the principles of the rat conditioning experiment on Snyder and their young victims. The purpose of the training was to get the victims to do what he wanted them to do. The ideal age was around fourteen or fifteen, Thornton said, young enough to be psychologically pliable. But instead of music, he used violence and fear.

He told Rea that he had intentionally conditioned Michelle to be compliant. Showing his gun to her was intended to serve as "the music" in Thornton's version of the laboratory experiment, and Michelle, like the other victims, was supposed to relax and eventually be unafraid whenever he displayed a gun.

Thornton chuckled about Snyder's flight after they returned home from the Tulsa shooting. Her fear, the very act of running away, all went according to his plan for her, Thornton said, which was more complicated. Preceding the Springer shooting, he had been grooming Snyder for two years and he had anticipated that she would run because she was scared. Snyder was exhibiting the stage of fearfulness, which was a necessary milestone in achieving traumatic bonding. Several months before, Snyder had seen extreme violence when they had drowned and cut up Jessie Peters, a young girl close to her own age, and then she had witnessed a bloody shooting of a helpless victim. Forced exposure to murder was intended to condition Snyder and numb her to violence. Thornton told her that it would also bond them together as a wolf pack. He made her participate by using a ruse to snatch Jessie from her home, by holding Jessie's hand and "comforting" her while Thornton raped her, and then by calming her down afterward as they sat on the bed. When the girl had settled down, Snyder suggested that she take a bath. She was compliant because Jessie trusted her and she went into the bathroom and got into the tub all by herself. Then came the drowning and the grisly disposal of the butchered body parts wired to cinderblocks.

Thornton was very proud of Snyder's actions because, according to him, that was how wolves hunted, as a pack. He had the power and authority and was the one instilling fear in the victim while Snyder would come to their rescue as their "savior." She related to the younger girls, acted as a friend, talked to them, and built their trust and confidence. Thornton wanted the victims to expect Snyder to save them in preparation for, as he put it, "when things changed to something worse." By that, he meant for when the time came for the victim to die. The first time he pulled out a gun, its purpose was to intimidate the victim. The second time was to make the victim feel comfortable around the weapon. Thornton's idea was to use Snyder to convince the victim to relax when the gun was around.

When he finally pulled out the gun to take the victim's life, Thornton said, "she wouldn't worry about it at the time. She would have a comfort zone" because she had been tricked. Thornton constructed the elaborate charade to make his victims relax while being assaulted and murdered.

After Snyder ran away in 1996, Thornton played the happy husband to Pamela for months, monitoring Snyder's locations via mutual friends who were part of his drug cabal. He waited until he decided that the time had come for him to pick up Snyder and bring her back. It was time to continue her training.

When she returned, Snyder started drawing. Thornton thought she was a talented artist, and he bought her supplies and hung her work on the wall. He was particularly proud of a sketch she did in pencil, depicting a daydreaming girl soaking in a bathtub. A dialogue bubble

floating over her head contained sawed body parts that
were manacled, chained, and dripping blood. A full-face
mask over the severed head revealed Thornton and Snyder's clever solution to the dilemma of how to affix a
cinderblock to a head.

Seven

The notes were in Snyder's round, childlike script:

> *4:53 Thursday . . . was past old road . . . was wearing*
> *shorts on a cold day . . . Had her same backpack . . .*

And on the next page:

> *960 Chollon*
> *Danielle—(dany) 338.3198. . . . .*
> *Last Name Cummins . . .*
> *I told her I was 15,*
> *Just moved up here, name is Chris*
> *1-21-98 Wednesday—her mom was there*
> *at around 3:00. her Moms car is a convertible*
> *Green car w/ Tan Top (an expensive looking car)*

Hudson, the father of a teenage daughter, cringed at the note further down the page:

She still walks home alone!!!

The green spiral notebook had haunted Hudson since he had unearthed it during the search of the Running Springs cabin months before. Hudson and sheriff's investigators spent nearly a week going through all of the houses owned by Thornton—the home in Blue Jay, the cabin in Running Springs, Thornton's mother's house in Mesa, Arizona, as well as the vehicles: the GMC camper, the Jeep Thornton left in Mesa, Pamela Bivens's pickup truck, and the brown Suburban. The forensic techs had barely begun to catalog and process the overwhelming amount of evidence, and Hudson had not even cherry-picked the most relevant items for further examination when he took a closer look at the notebook. The simple green notebook containing the girl's name, address, phone number jotted next to detailed description of her family's habits intrigued Hudson enough for him to make a mental note to return to the notebook at his earliest opportunity. The scribbles attained frightening significance after learning about the murder of Jessie Peters, who had been lured from her home in a similar fashion and when viewed in light of other items found in the Suburban—binoculars, maps, duct tape, cable ties, guns, and ammunition.

Hudson had been carrying a full caseload when Thornton and Snyder were captured and their case landed on his desk; he and sheriff's detectives were hip-deep in leads related to Michelle Curran's murder. And Hudson, who had unearthed the murder of Jessie Peters and the attempted murder of Sylvia Springer, was the sole investigator into those crimes. He didn't want too much time to go by before taking another look at that notebook to find out if there were additional victims beyond Michelle, Jessie, and Sylvia. He set aside an afternoon to review the notes in an examination room at the sheriff's department's cavernous evidence warehouse.

The Riverside County Sheriff's Department had two

huge, nondescript warehouses that they used to store thousands of pieces of evidence collected from crime scenes large and small, from petty thefts to multiple homicides. The Lake Elsinore facility had been built to handle the overflow from the warehouse at the sheriff's substation in Rubidoux. Years before, the county had instituted a bar code system to streamline the identification, organization, and retrieval of evidence. Evidence was tagged with a bar code sticker containing the names of the evidence tech and the detective, the case number, and a brief description of the item. After the code was scanned into a computer with a hand-held scanner, one sticker was placed on the bag containing the evidence item and an identical sticker was affixed to the master list of evidence. Once the item arrived at the warehouse, technicians used the bar codes to store and, when required, to locate the item. Hudson had called ahead and gave the evidence techs the bar code for the notebook so that he could view it in the evidence room.

Hudson opened the spiral journal. Notes on the first page in Snyder's scrawl were about a pair of hitchhikers on Pedley Street near Sixth Street and Waterman: Lena, fifteen, and Brandy, seventeen, who wore eyeglasses. Snyder noted that she told them that her "sister's" name was Theresa and her "uncle's" name was John. But without a detailed description, last name, or contact information, "Lena" and "Brandy" would be impossible to track down. The next series of notes in Snyder's handwriting pertained to the comings and goings of people who rented property in the area, the vehicles they drove, when they let the dogs out, and when they went to bed.

A surveillance of hitchhikers and renters was creepy but not criminal. Hudson was more interested in their next subject, a girl who lived near Thornton and Snyder in the Lake Arrowhead area. They stalked their prey and kept a detailed log of her habits. After learning from Angela and Pamela in Las Vegas about additional victims, Hudson knew that Thornton and Snyder were serial offenders. The notes told him the frightening extent to which they conducted meticulous research. As he had with the Jessie Peters murder, Thornton had sent Snyder to interact with the girl at her bus stop, according to her notebook. Then she watched the girl walk to and from her home, and recorded her comings and goings from the house. The log had the victim's last name, phone number, home address, the members of her household, the make and model of vehicles coming and going from the house, her mother's work schedule, when the girl usually got home and when her mother arrived home from work. The detailed entries with dates and times were in both Thornton's and Snyder's handwriting.

Their notes read like a dossier: Danyelle Cummins started seventh grade in September 1997. She turned twelve on January 17, 1998. She lived in Crestline, a mountain community in the San Bernardino Mountains near the towns of Running Springs, Blue Jay, Twin Peaks, and Lake Arrowhead. The less populated mountain area had fewer schools and just one junior high school, Mary Putnam Hank Middle School, which Danyelle attended. Lake Gregory was approximately two miles from her home. Her parents were divorced and she lived with her mother and stepfather, her younger brothers, and a younger sister, Mallory Rebecca Cummins, who went by her middle name Rebecca. Danyelle was sixteen months older than Mallory Rebecca. Danyelle's mother worked in Santa Ana and drove a green convertible Sebring Chrysler with a tan top. Her stepfather drove a white Dodge pickup truck. Danyelle helped get her brothers and sister ready for school, and made sure the house was clean and that the kids had done their homework.

Danyelle, Snyder wrote, "was pissed because she had to clean house, possibly every day." But Snyder apparently got close enough to check her progress.

"House looked like a pig stye!!! 'But' shes suppose [*sic*] to have house clean before mom gets home," Snyder wrote.

Danyelle's mother expected her to do her chores, but she didn't like it, "especially the dishes." Danyelle's biological father had custody of the children every other weekend, but he didn't always show up. He sometimes drove a burgundy Honda, sometimes a white Dodge Omni.

Danyelle walked to the bus stop every morning and rode the bus to school, then walked home again from the bus stop after school. The bus trip was between forty-five minutes to an hour, then it was a two-mile walk home. It usually took Danyelle forty-five minutes to walk home from the bus stop, so she would arrive at home between 4 and 5 p.m., depending on whether she walked home with friends. Sometimes she was late, "due to (foggy) weather." She usually took the old, washed-out road behind their house, which was shorter, though it was a steep incline. In winter, even with snow on the ground, Danyelle still preferred to wear either shorts or skirts.

Armed with the address listed in the journal, a last name, and a vehicle description and license number, Hudson did a background check and found out that the house had been sold a couple of years before. Hudson gleaned from records from the local middle school, the post office, and the real estate agent who had handled the transaction that a family by the name of Cummins had lived at 960 Chillon Street in Crestline in 1998 during the time period of Thornton's and Snyder's surveillance. The community of Crestline was about five miles down Highway 189 from where Thornton and Snyder had lived in Blue Jay. Hudson found a current address for the Cummins family in Hesperia. He phoned the mother, and he and Rushton drove there to find out what had happened to her little girl.

Mrs. Cummins invited Hudson and Rushton inside and took them straight through to the backyard, where the two men in suits found themselves in the midst of a summer swimming party surrounded by school-age children clad in bathing suits. She introduced them to Danyelle, who had light brown hair and was small and slender, similar in build to the other victims. Her full name was Danyelle Fonda Cummins; her nickname was indeed, as recorded in the spiral notebook, Dany. When they lived at that address, their phone number was, as Snyder had noted, 338-3198. Danyelle's mother confirmed that she and her father were divorced. she had primary custody of their children and acknowledged the details of custody arrangement and visitation, the makes and models of their vehicles, Danyelle's route back and forth to school, and the kind of clothing Danyelle wore—shorts and skirts even with snow on the ground. Danyelle volunteered when Hudson and Rushton interviewed her that she had chores after school, which she still disliked. Both Danyelle and her mother acknowledged that their busy household with a divorced, working mother and three children sometimes resembled a pig sty, as Snyder had noted.

Rushton asked Danyelle whether she recalled a young lady asking her personal questions. She did remember an "odd" episode when she was in middle school in Crestline. She said that for a time, a girl was dropped off each morning at the bus stop by her "uncle," but the new girl never boarded the bus and Danyelle never saw her at school. Danyelle assumed that the girl was just ditching. The girl said she was fifteen, but looked older. This girl asked Danyelle a lot of questions but didn't talk to the other kids. She dressed in "slutty clothing," had long blond hair and blue eyes, and was "really skinny with a cute body." She stood about five feet, three inches. Danyelle was puzzled about why the girl was dropped off at the bus stop when her uncle could have driven her to school. Danyelle and her mother confirmed that Danyelle had taken the #26 bus with a male bus driver.

She had been twelve years old when Snyder had introduced herself at the bus stop. At the time, Snyder had been seventeen. Danyelle didn't recognize photos of either Thornton or Snyder, but she confirmed that the girl who had spoken with her matched Snyder's description.

Once Hudson and Rushton reviewed the notes, Danyelle asked why they were asking so many questions. Hudson gently informed her that "some people may have been watching you." Rushton told Danyelle and her mother about Thornton and Snyder and why they had been arrested. Danyelle's mother said that the family had moved to Hesperia in the summer of 1998, meaning that they had moved before Thornton and Snyder had had a chance to abduct Danyelle.

Danyelle sat in silence as the seriousness of the situation, which had been grave enough to bring a prosecutor and a district attorney investigator to her house years after the fact, began to register. The young girl's body shook as tears rolled down her face. Her mother leaned over and held her daughter as she sobbed. Hudson and Rushton consoled her and reassured her that they would do everything possible to prevent Thornton and Snyder from getting out of jail.

After their visit, the emotional aftershock of learning that she had been targeted by a pair of serial killers had severely upset Danyelle. Her mother called Hudson to let him know that her daughter was still upset. She sought counseling for her, and continued to keep Hudson appraised about her daughter's progress.

Hudson was glad that they hadn't told Danyelle and her mother *everything* in the notebook. In the pages that followed was a list of 221 questions. Numbers 1 to 126 had been written by Thornton, and numbers 127 to 221 had been written by Snyder. The items were pragmatic and methodical, almost like a patient intake or questionnaire.

1. Last name, Middle, First. Phone #.
2. Birthday/Born where
3. Grade/A B C D F
4. Address.
5. Who lives in your house?

6. Mom/Age/Name
   Dad/Age/Name
   Girlfriend/Boyfriend live in? Or Date?
   Sis / Bro-Age/Name
7. Mother work? Dad work?
8. Cars? Pets?
9. Favorite color?

At first glance, the questions appear to be a simple list of subjects to start small talk.

What's your name? What's your birthday? Do you live around here? Do you live with your parents? Are you a good student? Do you have a pet? Do you belong to any clubs? Do you like to paint, or play piano?

More than one nervous guy apprehensive about meeting girls might compile such a list of conversation starters. But as Hudson scanned the list, he saw that the questions quickly turned personal. *Do you have your own bedroom? Do you sleep alone? What do you wear to bed? What's your bed time? Do you have a boyfriend? Have you ever been kissed by a boy? Do you wear a bra? Do you always wear one? What color?*

Hudson continued through the list and saw that Thornton was creating questions to identify risk-takers.

How many times is [sic] ears pierced? Are there other parts of your body you want pierced? (nose, eyebrow, belly button, lip, tongue, etc.) Smoke cigs? Do you have any tattoos? Do you like to go to parties? Do you ever ditch school? Do you ever sneak out after bed time? Ever get detention? Why? Have the police ever been called on you? Have you met a lot of boys or girls? Your age or older or younger? Do you buy cable, or do you

steal TV? Does your mom do drugs or drink? Do
you talk back to adults (mom etc) alot? Are you al-
lowed to weare [sic] your make-up, hair & clothes
how you want?

Hudson knew that youngsters who tended to be rebellious were easy prey, as well as victims whose families
were in turmoil. Apparently Thornton had created questions to screen for that as well.

Do you get into trouble at school? Do you get into
trouble at home? Do you have a curfew? Do you
fight with your parents? When was the last fight,
what about? Do you ever get tired of being checked
up on? Do they punish you—slap, spank, yell, re-
strict? What do your parents do when you lie to
them? Do you ever get detention? Do you talk back
to adults (mom etc.) a lot? Do you ever find drugs or
mom's playtoys in her bedroom? Do you look
through her stuff a lot?

Hudson saw that Thornton had the sophistication to
inquire about the other end of the family spectrum to assess their familial resources.

Do you get in trouble for calling your parents at
work? How many relatives do you have? Do you
have a lot of friends? Any relatives who are rich/
wealthy in the family? Who? Who do you eat lunch
with? Do you have aunts, uncles, cousins? Where
do they live—what do they do? (Sssh cops?)

Thornton was testing a potential victim's connections
to friends as well as family, noted by the "sssh cops"
aside, which seemed to indicate that he would be cautious if any of their intended victims had relatives in law
enforcement. Hudson wondered where he got the questions; some of them read like a psychological assessment.

*Do you like to follow or lead and have others fol-
low? Do you like doing whatever it takes to fit in
with pals, etc.? Do you ever get teased at school/
home? Do you like getting an attitude with people?
How much time do you spend with your friends?
What kinds of things do you tend to have a problem
with—i.e.—memory, lazy, always late, too shy. Do
you keep your room clean? Do you think that
"your" [sic] psyshic?*

Taken as a whole, the questions revealed a sophisti-
cated psychological strategy designed to determine a victim's willingness to be enticed or pressured with the
promise of drugs or a party; to see if she was amenable to
getting into a stranger's car; if the victim was detached
from family and friends; if she was accessible in or near
her home.

*How many rooms in your house? Do you keep your
window, door open or closed (in bedroom) at
night? Do you walk up and down your street often?
To get away from whom? Do you ever get driven to/
from school? Do you ever sneak out after bed time?
Have you ever hitchhiked? How far away from
home allowed to go without asking?*

Hudson thought the questions composed a script to
abduct girls. Thornton and Snyder had written an operating manual for getting their victims to divulge private information in order to gain their confidence and lure them
away. The target was being tested for susceptibility, and
Snyder was the tool for that. Even if they had captured a
victim, several questions were listed that assessed their
resourcefulness to escape, as Thornton put it, or whether
they were compliant enough to not try running away:

*Do you have a computer? Do you know how to use
a phone book? Ever call the police on someone?*

Do you have your own bank account? Do you ever watch McGiver (escape artist) [sic]?

Several of the questions reflected a fantasy that Thornton wanted from the girls and perhaps contained a hint of what was to come.

Do you bruise easily? Have you ever been beat up? Ever wanted to take nude (or not nude) photos of yourself and put them on computer or in magazines? Are there any guns in the house? Do you have a favorite kind of animal? Do you like or are you afraid of wolves? Have you ever thought about committing a crime, murder, robbery, breaking & entering,—ever commit a crime? With who? Whose idea? Did you enjoy it or not? Have you ever seen a(n) (X-rated) film? How do you feel about Death?

Hudson thought Thornton's questions read like something out of *Helter Skelter*, a page from the Charles Manson family history. Thornton and Snyder sought total control over their victims. He recognized several questions that he believed specifically targeted Danyelle, although Thornton could use them for other local victims.

Ever see old friends at Old Town? Must be a bitch on [the] hill w/snow on the ground? Do you feed the blue Jays, Squirels [sic]? Do you exercise (besides all that dam walking up that Big hill street Shhh!!! Shhh Shhh!!!! Strength???

Hudson thought that the shushing was Thornton's childish way of indicating that they shouldn't write too much in their generic questions about someone that they were actively pursuing.

After reading the handwritten questions, Hudson reviewed the timeline of the various cases. Jessie Peters was kidnapped and killed in March 1996. Sylvia Springer was shot in October 1996. The surveillance of Danyelle occurred for several months starting in January 1998. Michelle Curran was kidnapped and killed in 2001. That left a few years for the couple to practice honing their technique.

Following the questions was a final collection of notes. The final page, in Snyder's handwriting, was titled *"Things About Adoption !!!"* The notes contained details about overseas adoptions, statistics on the number of adoptions in the United States and Europe, information about prospective parents, and tips for successful adoption: *"They want parents who Plan on adopting to Educate themselves first, do home study . . . Make Sure they want to take the risk with intercountry adoption check background for seperation* [sic]*, loss, or greef* [sic]*."*

As he thumbed through the worn green notebook, Hudson knew that it represented valuable evidence, but he was disturbed by the knowledge that he was holding in his hands a how-to manual for gaining the confidence of a victims in order to abduct them. Hudson wasn't certain yet how Thornton and Snyder's ideas about adoption figured into their criminal activity. Hudson didn't think that Thornton was looking to adopt a child. Whatever the details of the adoption scheme, Hudson knew it had something to do with murder.

Robert Presley Detention Center
Riverside, California
January 2003

Every time Thornton returned from court, he'd have a good laugh. He wasn't surprised that investigators were going after him, he was amused because they had no idea about the other crimes he and Snyder had committed. He had heard tidbits of what Hudson had unearthed from his defense attorney at court that day.

"They might get close, but they'll never find out," Thornton gloated to Rea "They won't solve it. Some of them will be retired by the time they figure it out. If they ever figure it out."

The police, Thornton told Rea as he shuffled cards, would be chasing leads about their crimes for years. He took pride in having deliberately planned for all possible outcomes. As long as they stuck to his plan, Thornton boasted, they would walk out of jail. He planned everything. For example, he had even rehearsed with Snyder what they would do in the event they were chased by police: they would split up and Snyder was supposed to flag down a motorist and claim she was fleeing attackers.

Thornton constantly reminded Rea that he had used mind control techniques to brainwash Snyder. He chose young teenage girls the same way that he had selected Snyder, by assessing whether they would be susceptible to being conditioned. He enjoyed controlling them and getting them to do what he wanted. Maintaining control was part of his plan, he told Rea, but it was not his final plan.

Snyder's reaction to the murders and the act of running away went according to the plan Thornton had set in motion during the two years he had been grooming her: establishing himself as her father-authority figure.

"A father figure with benefits," Thornton said. "Look at her. She is trained. She does what I want her to do."

He instilled fear, alternated by giving rewards. So when Thornton found Snyder and brought her back after her flight, he bought her a house.

When they bought the Running Springs cabin, Thornton suggested to his wife that they use it as a vacation rental. What he failed to mention was that he intended to give the house to Snyder. This, too, was part of his plan. Following his campaign of exposing Snyder to bloody violence, the next step was to isolate her in a remote mountain cabin and make himself her sole social contact and her most powerful influence. Thornton gave her several tasks. She was to study their training film, *Natural Born Killers*. She was to write a list of questions to initiate conversations with prospective victims. And, she was to research and compile statistics on adoptions. Lastly, Thornton gave her a more physical task.

Thornton handed Snyder a shovel and told her to dig a tunnel into the hillside underneath the stairs. They were going to create a secret room to fulfill his terrifying vision: using Snyder as a lure, they would kidnap young women and imprison them in the secret basement room. There, Thornton would rape and impregnate them. Once the babies were born, he planned to make money by selling the babies to parents desperate to adopt an infant.

Eight

Pamela Thornton was on the phone with a friend when she heard footsteps behind her. Before she could turn around, she heard the soft click of a trigger and felt the cold steel of a gun barrel at the back of her head. It was Thornton.

"Drop the phone."

She did.

"Do you want a divorce?" he asked.

She stood frozen as the man she had loved for more than twenty years pushed the gun to her head.

"Do you?" he shouted.

They had raised a family, started up a very successful business, and gone through some tough times. She had been both his sounding board and, at times, his punching bag. She didn't want to be physically or mentally abused any more. Pamela was tired of being afraid all the time. She knew Thornton was capable of killing her. Had it come down to this? Did he want to kill her?

Pamela held her breath for a moment.

"Yes," she said, "I want a divorce."

She felt him hesitate. Pamela was shaking.

"What if I don't want to give you one?" he muttered.

Pamela knew her husband well enough to know that this was his adolescent side talking. She had called his bluff, and the moment she stood up to him, he backed down. She had leveled the playing field.

"I want one anyway," Pamela said.

"You can't divorce me," he said slowly, pulling the gun away from her head and walking past her into the bathroom.

"If you divorce me, I'll kill myself," he said. Then he shut the door and locked himself in.

Pamela was stunned. She had long been on the receiving end of Thornton's mind games—he studied psychological coercion—but she had never seen him like this. Was threatening to kill himself another way to get her to do what he wanted? Thornton had never before mentioned suicide; she believed he would do it.

So the tables were turned. She leaned against the bathroom door, slumping under the emotional strain. Despite her husband's relationship with Janeen Snyder, his drug addiction, his abandonment of the business and of her, and the constant physical and verbal abuse culminating with her staring down the barrel of a gun, Pamela found herself comforting Thornton, pleading with him through the closed bathroom door not to hurt himself. As with their other abusive encounters, she was the one in tears.

Pamela reflected on how their lives had crumbled in the past year. Was it her husband's drug use or his relationship with Janeen Snyder that had driven them to this point? Did they even have a marriage anymore?

Thornton had moved Snyder into the Running Springs cabin, even though he had told Pamela that they would use it as a vacation rental. Snyder had papered the cabin walls with her blood-smeared artwork. Pamela never lived in the cabin. Thornton had moved out of the Blue Jay home he had shared with Pamela and into the cabin with

Snyder just a few miles away. Thornton now split his time between the two households, and his two women.

Lonely and starved for attention, Pamela had ventured online and started a conversation with a gentleman in an Internet chat room. Rene Pardo was a charming and successful computer software developer who took an interest in Pamela, who admitted to being fortysomething and separated from her husband. They called each other by their screen names: "Mr. Newbie" for Pardo and "PKLady" for Pamela, shorthand for Pamela Kay. She considered the online flirting harmless since Pardo lived in Toronto, but Pardo said he would be in Los Angeles in early December for business. She had never before met anyone online or cheated on her husband, even though he was sharing a household with Snyder. Pamela took the initiative and asked if they could meet. A part of her felt guilty and a little saddened, but she also felt excited by meeting someone who took a genuine interest in her. It was the happiest she had felt in months.

She dressed up and made the hour-and-a-half-long trip from Blue Jay into downtown Los Angeles to the Sheraton hotel. Pamela beamed when she met the Swiss-born Pardo, who had glasses, an easy smile, and a sweep of dark brown hair across his forehead. He was attentive and well-read, and before long, they retired to his room. Afterward, he walked her to her car and they parted ways. Pamela felt as if she were floating all the way home. It was the positive boost she needed to make a break from Thornton. She kept in touch with Pardo over the holidays with instant messages and phone calls, and they discussed getting together again when he returned to Los Angeles. On January 2, he contacted Pamela to let her know he had arrived. Pardo got a return phone call, but it wasn't from Pamela.

"This is Mikey," said a calm male voice. "Pam's husband. Your affair is over."

Pardo told Thornton that he would be willing to meet with him to work things out. Thornton agreed and calmly told Pardo that he would enjoy a road trip to Canada, where he would spend three days torturing him, his wife, and their daughters and then "bring back his body parts." In fear for his life, Pardo immediately changed hotel rooms, then called Pamela and left a message asking what they should do. She returned his call twenty minutes later, her voice tight as she relayed a message from "Mikey."

"Michael's a hit man," Pamela said, adding that he typically charged $25,000 to kill people but would charge Pardo one additional dollar to spare his life. For $25,001, Thornton would agree not to kill him, and the dollar was "because I'm a whore," Pamela told Pardo. Shortly after midnight, Pardo received an instant message from PKLady on his laptop computer.

"Ever see a pig butchered . . . real slow . . . up close?" the message read. There was little question that the threat came from Thornton. Pardo also thought there was little question that Thornton intended to kill him and that a meeting with him would not end well. In a subsequent e-mail, Thornton wrote: "Guess you didn't want to talk face-to-face after all. You did get to fuck my wife!!! Wonder what your wife and daughters would think of you? Wondering how you'd feel if the same happened to all of them, Hmmmmm?"

The next day, Pardo reported the phone call and the threats to the FBI and the Los Angeles Police Department. Thornton continued to send threats to Pardo, using e-mail rather than the PKLady chat box, but the sender's own e-mail address was blocked. Pardo was unnerved by the messages, particularly by the e-mail that contained his home address and former addresses, the addresses of Pardo's businesses, his handful of e-mail addresses, the name of his business partner, his educational history, and details about his post-graduate work at Harvard. He considered it the equivalent of a Mafia hit man mailing his intended victim a photo of their children to show that he knew where they lived.

Ironically, Pardo was one of the software engineers who had developed the early versions of instant messaging. Even though he knew that Thornton had sent the messages, he had little beyond the phone call dialogue and the instant message to show law enforcement. He used his computer expertise to trace the computer user who had masked his own address. To his surprise, Pardo found that he was not dealing with a casual computer hobbyist. Thornton had quickly unearthed personal information about Pardo then routed his threatening e-mails through multiple servers to mask his identity, an astonishing level of sophistication for current times, much less for 1999. When Pardo returned to Toronto, a fresh e-mail was waiting: "How was your stay? Get all you wanted . . . hmmmmm? Call anybody you want, you dumb fuck. Makes no difference to me. As you saw, fucker, I'd be a very careful fellow. Of course, I told you what I wanted from you. I think I'll let them fuck you for a while then we, like you asked for, can have a face-to-face. I don't give a fuck weather [*sic*] you pay up or not mother-fucker. Like I told you on the phone, the three days I spend on you will be lots of fun. Sounds like a real good time. Be seeing you."

Pardo believed Thornton would gladly take his money, then kill him. As an anonymous sender, Thornton e-mailed Pardo a widely distributed poem that Thornton lifted word-for-word from a website that used black humor for stress management. Called "Serenity," it describes a cool, clear stream in a "secret . . . secluded" mountain area where "the water below you is still and clear. You can easily make out the face of the person whose head you are holding under water [emphasis added]."

"There now . . . feeling better???" the poem ended. Thornton added, "Wanta [*sic*] play Rene???"

Faced with the choice of either paying $25,001 or being killed, Pardo told Thornton that he was happy to pay, though he continued to cooperate with authorities in the United States as well as with Canadian law enforcement.

He had also hired a private investigator to find out what he could about Thornton. Despite Pardo's willingness to pay, Thornton apparently was more interested in exacting his revenge than the cash, and he continued to electronically taunt Pardo. Pardo repeatedly hacked into Thornton's server in an attempt to identify his e-mail addresses. He finally found several, including a curious address: in10d-2dv8u@earthlink.net. He studied it for a while until he figured out the meaning by sounding it out: "Intend to deviate you."

Despite the turmoil, Pardo continued to be very kind to Pamela. If his own life was in danger, he feared even more for hers and encouraged her to leave Thornton. Like many abused women who are often unwilling to leave abusive men from whom they receive the smallest scraps of affection, Pamela was reluctant to close the door completely on the marriage. Pardo suggested that she could simply move to another of their homes. Consumed with anger over her affair, Thornton busied himself with dishing out electronic threats to Pardo. That gave her time to move from the Blue Jay home and into their first house in the Rialto suburbs.

Far from her husband's fists, she felt calmer and slept more peacefully. She confided in Pardo that she was better off without Thornton. The more time she spent away from her husband, the more she mustered the strength to leave him for good. She wasn't calling him anymore to ask any questions about the business, and once Thornton sensed she was pulling away, he visited Rialto, seeking to assert control over her at the point of a gun. From the other side of the bathroom door, she found herself on familiar terrain of emotional upheaval. In a flood of tears, she promised Thornton that she wouldn't divorce him, and he finally emerged from the bathroom. Days after the drama subsided and Thornton got what he wanted, she broke under the strain. She was crying uncontrollably, couldn't sleep, and couldn't stop shaking. She was hospitalized for several days for a nervous breakdown and was treated with a cocktail of anti-depressants, anti-anxiety medication, a tranquilizer, and sleeping pills. Angela, her boyfriend, and their baby moved into the Rialto home to take care of Pamela. And despite Pamela's intense fear of her husband, he drove down from the Running Springs cabin every few days to "check in on her." He began spending more time with her and by spring, he had moved back in.

As she recovered after her hospital stay, the two had a long talk. He acknowledged that he was an addict, and Pamela encouraged him to get some help. But she knew in her heart that he wouldn't do it because he didn't want to quit. And it wasn't long before he moved Snyder into the house, too. Now Pamela, Thornton, Snyder, Angela, her boyfriend, and their baby were all living under one roof. Angela tried to convince her mother to leave Thornton, but Pamela was in no frame of mind to stand up to him. Aware of the deep dysfunction surrounding them, Angela and her family moved out. Pamela eventually regained her footing, and with it the uneasy equilibrium of living in the same household as her husband's much younger mistress. She busied herself with the salons while Thornton dabbled on his three computers and tended to his growing drug habit. When she came home after working all day, she found strangers hanging around and her house in a dismal state of disarray. Her fear of her husband meant she didn't dare to ask him to quit drugs. Any conversations with Thornton about their business, the state of the household, and the state of their relationship ended with him waving her away.

"Go take a pill, Pam," he'd say. "Go take a pill."

When Pamela insisted, Thornton resorted to violence. One day she tried to run away from him. He chased her down the hallway and slapped her so hard that he left a handprint on her thigh. She risked angering Thornton by pressing him about his relationship with Snyder, but he continued to deny it. Living in the same household with Thornton made Pamela feel unsafe. She felt as if she was in limbo. Though she was clearly unwanted, he couldn't let her go.

Thornton spent his days with Snyder but was no kinder to her than he was to Pamela. He yelled at her for "little stupid stuff" and was quick to anger when she didn't perform a task correctly or as quickly as he liked. During the day, the Rialto home devolved into a meth pad where Thornton and Snyder's friends took drugs and hung out.

Pamela welcomed the quiet that came when Thornton and Snyder traveled; she was happier when he wasn't around to hurt her. By the summer of 1999, Thornton's attacks on Pamela averaged one incident per week and the amount of force he used was escalating. Snyder sometimes jumped in to yank Thornton off Pamela at the risk of his turning violent toward her. Once when Thornton pinned Pamela to the sofa, Snyder tackled him to prevent him from burning her with his cigarette. Each time Thornton and Snyder went out of town, Pamela used the time away from her husband to emotionally prepare herself to leave him, but she was frightened. Would he track her down? Would he do to her what he said he had done to his other victims?

As the months went by, Thornton and Snyder began to act openly as a couple in front of Pamela. They did not display a romantic liaison, but they clearly had ended their father-daughter type of relationship. Thornton's denials about Snyder to Pamela were running hollow: The couple was inseparable. He spent almost all of his time with Snyder, on his laptop computer, or using drugs. By his own choice, Thornton had stopped being intimate with Pamela, and their marriage, like the business, was faltering. Pamela clung to the slender tendril that remained of their marriage. She still loved her husband, and Thornton knew that he could twist her devotion to him and manipulate her to do things for him. This distortion in their relationship—the manipulator and the woman clinging to love in spite of his bald manipulation—had kept them together all of these years. He knew that she would never divorce him.

Or so he thought.

A year after Pamela's short-lived affair with Rene Pardo, Thornton, Snyder, and Pamela went to Las Vegas to celebrate Thornton's birthday in early December. Thornton and Snyder drove out while Pamela stayed behind to wrap up business. She flew out and joined them at the Stratosphere hotel on December 6, where they all stayed in one room. After a night at the casino, Thornton gave his wife a gambling token, then went downstairs to purchase a Diet Pepsi from a vending machine. But when he inserted the coins, the wrong soda came out. Thornton downed Diet Pepsi by the bucketful and disliked all other sodas. Agitated from his long-term drug use, Thornton banged on the machine from irritation. He asked Pamela for the token he had given her, but she had misplaced it. This enraged Thornton because he now had the wrong soda and no coins left to buy his Diet Pepsi. When they returned to their room, Thornton gave Pamela a beating. He hit her and threw her against the wall. Lunging at her, he wrapped his hands around her neck. At one point, he straddled her and choked her on the bed. Exhausted from the battle and gasping for breath, she could no longer fight him off and she went limp, allowing him to choke her. Snyder jumped on his back, pulled him off Pamela and coaxed him to go downstairs to the casino to cool off. Bruised and sore around her neck, Pamela cried herself to sleep. The next day, Thornton was still angry with Pamela, who was in pain from the beating the night before. All three of them went to the lookout on top of the Stratosphere, and Thornton suddenly punched Pamela in the face for no apparent reason.

This was the last straw. Pamela didn't want to be part of this threesome any longer. She went back to their room, threw her things into her bag, grabbed a taxi to the airport, and booked a plane home. On her husband's birthday,

Pamela returned to California and walked into a domestic violence shelter with a black eye, handprints on her neck, and numerous bruises.

Weeks later, Thornton and Snyder celebrated their partnership and the holiday season. Snyder made Thornton a card out of flimsy college-ruled paper. The green and yellow felt-tipped marker leaked through the thin paper, making it difficult to read:

> *"Merry Xmas Partner . . . And a Happy New, [sic] well heres [sic] a brand new year for me—(us) to make Rewardable and On the Road to our future [happy face] Lets do it, Millenium [sic] -With a certain person leaving is so good to be true. It fell In our laps, how perfect is that!! . . . Now lets see what happens next! I'm excited, how bout you? I love you 4ever. Me."*

Robert Presley Detention Center
Riverside, California
January 2003

"Their kitten Missy was at their home in Lake Arrowhead and even with the extra food that had been left out for her, she was probably running low so they needed to get back to care for her."

"How does that sound?" Thornton asked.

"O.K.," Rea said cautiously. "Go on."

Thornton wanted Rea's feedback on that section. The letter was written as if someone else besides Thornton and Snyder were the author, and he had used initials instead of names. He wrote that he and Snyder were having "lousy luck" after a few days in Las Vegas and they drove around town on their final morning contemplating "the possibility of buying some marijuana."

Within the hour, he wrote, "JS suddenly told MT to

pull over. After a short conversation with someone out her open window the rear passenger door opened and in jumped a pretty white female with dark hair."

Rea realized that this was the girl that Thornton and Snyder were accused of killing. As Thornton read the story he had concocted, he told Rea what really happened. There was no 7:30 a.m. drug run. They weren't looking for marijuana, Thornton said, they were cruising for a victim. He had driven to an area where they could find a girl like Michelle. Thornton spotted her because he thought she was very "different looking," and told Snyder to get her. Snyder said something outside of the car window first, then got out of the car and asked her if she knew anyone who had drugs. Using the questions she had practiced on many victims, Snyder played her usual role as bait and lured Michelle into the backseat of the Suburban.

The two girls were "instant best friends," Thornton wrote, and when Snyder said "it was a shame they didn't meet until their last day in town," their new dark-haired friend begged them to take her with them to visit a boyfriend in Monterey, California. Responsible adults, Thornton and Snyder agreed to give her a ride "only after" she assured them that she was eighteen.

There was no boyfriend in Monterey. Thornton told Rea he made that up. He trained a weapon on Michelle the moment she climbed into the backseat, then watched her reaction. It was the first step to gain control of her. He was pleased to see that she was "mentally weak," meaning she would be easy to control. Thornton said that she went with them at the point of a gun and never wanted to go to Monterey or anywhere else with them.

Thornton invented a plot twist for the letter: "They [Thornton and Snyder] informed her of the danger they heard from two men named Tracy and Orlando, and they also made sure that she didn't have a problem with the fact that they used methamphetamine," wrote

Thornton. Despite copious spelling and grammatical errors in his letter, he spelled "methamphetamine" correctly.

"MC indicated that she understood about . . . the danger. She also said that she used Meth herself and it was at that point that the girls, sitting in the back seat together, smoked some Meth while MT drove back to the Best Western Motel."

Like a hack fiction writer, Thornton was setting up a straw man—or men in this case—to blame for Michelle's murder. There was no Orlando. Thornton did have a drug buddy named Tracy, who he wanted to link to this murder as payback for a feud.

He told Rea that he gave Michelle drugs to control her: methamphetamine to keep her alert and marijuana to make her calm. He controlled the amount that he gave her—not too much, not too little—for the effect he wanted. The drugs served a secondary purpose of altering the victim's mind as well as getting her addicted. A drug habit was an effective control mechanism, spawning a dependence upon Thornton to satisfy it. He set up the victims so that they would need him.

"After they got to the motel they packed, loaded the Suburban, checked out, and left together for California," Thornton wrote.

Thornton left the pages with Rea, who looked them over before copying them later in his own handwriting. He thought that Thornton left out the most important part. Thornton and Snyder had a plan to take Michelle Curran's life from the very moment she got into their car in Las Vegas. Thornton wanted Snyder to know how killing feels and understand what he felt when he killed someone. He wanted to share that intense experience with her. He thought it would bring them closer together and further intensify their bond.

Thornton told Rea about their "other victim," the one they didn't like to talk about. The other victim was what Thornton called "a failed trial run," and Thornton wouldn't tolerate another failure.

Michelle had to die.

Since Thornton considered this an important cornerstone of Snyder's training, he periodically flipped on his digital audio recorder to record Snyder's progress with her victim.

Nine

Rialto, California
February 2000

Michael Thornton woke up angry.

Smoking methamphetamine for days made for an agitated mood when the immediate euphoric effect of the drug wore off. He wandered out to the kitchen and tore open the refrigerator door. He wasn't rummaging for food but Diet Pepsi. *His* Diet Pepsi.

"Where's my Pepsi?" he bellowed. "Who drank my Pepsi? *Where is my Pepsi*!!!"

Furious, Thornton pulled out the gun he carried in the waistband of his pants and ran from room to room, waving the loaded weapon in the faces of his sleepy housemates.

"That was *my* Pepsi! *Who drank it?*" he yelled, "*You?* Did you take it?"

A den of meth users, barely out of their teens, inhabited the former Thornton family residence. They quietly picked up their belongings and tiptoed out of the house while Thornton thundered around looking for his long-gone soda. They moved back a few days later, the bizarre episode forgotten in a puff of meth.

The cast of characters on Silver Circle Street congregated near the drugs and the skinny dealer, Bobby Munoz, whose oversized shirts hung untucked over waspish hips that barely held up his enormous pants. At twenty-five, Munoz had dealt drugs out of his mother's house before moving in with Thornton, whom he knew through Alan Jiminez, Angela Thornton's boyfriend and one of his customers. Munoz attracted dealers and another half a dozen users who drifted in and out. They stayed a few nights or a few months. To all who passed though his front door, the middle-aged, bespectacled Thornton cultivated a "gangsta" image of himself. He and Snyder sometimes wore their matching long, black trenchcoats when they were "going mobbing." He took pride in having a girlfriend far younger than he.

Thornton let Munoz sell drugs out of the house and keep the proceeds as long as he and Snyder could use his meth whenever they wanted. Munoz was so addicted to meth that he would do just about anything to get high; even Thornton's gun-waving tantrum didn't faze him. The couple both carried loaded guns around the house. Thornton's was in his waistband and Snyder's—a tiny, two-shot Derringer smaller than a man's hand—was tucked in her purse. Despite his high-risk profession selling street drugs, Munoz didn't own a gun. He liked living at the house. Sometimes he, Thornton, and Snyder would get wired, raid one of the salons for cash, and blow it all at a local Indian casino.

At forty-four, Thornton enjoyed playing Peter Pan to a Neverland warren of post-adolescent addicts. There were no rules and no responsibilities. They did whatever they wanted whenever they wanted—which consisted primarily of laying around the house all day and night taking drugs. Everything was better when they were high. Meth is a strong stimulant that enables users to stay awake and alert for days, "tweaking" the whole time. Tweaking is nervous fiddling, which often includes performing tasks that normally aren't mentally engaging but appear intriguing when under the influence of the drug. When Thornton was tweaking, he worked on his computer. Snyder did beadwork and art, made jewelry, and cleaned the house. The initial euphoria lasted twenty to thirty minutes. After the euphoria fizzled, the strong stimulant effect remained. The more meth they used, the more they needed in order to maintain the intensity of the euphoria. When they came down, every little thing was irritating to Thornton, and his nest of users got on his nerves. As a chronic user, Thornton could sleep after using meth and Munoz learned to make himself scarce when Thornton woke up because he would find everything and everyone annoying until his next dose.

For that and other reasons, Munoz conducted his drug business outside the house. When a customer arrived, he met them at the front door, then directed them to a secluded spot away from the house to exchange money and drugs. When he saw that Thornton and Snyder had invited a young girl to the house one day, he didn't like it. The girl was there the next day and the following night, and it appeared as if she was there to stay. Munoz told Thornton she shouldn't stay at the house, because she was too young. He tried to explain to Thornton that having an underaged girl at the house where he was selling drugs would bring "heat" or police, and interfere with his drug business. It was bad for business, and he wanted the girl out.

Thornton did not agree. It was his house, his rules.

The girl stayed.

Robert Presley Detention Center
Riverside, California
January 2003

The more Thornton told Rea about his case and the more details he divulged about what they had done to Michelle, the more uncomfortable Rea became. Life behind bars was stressful enough, and even though he wanted to continue gathering information from Thornton, he found it difficult to continue keeping his facial expressions neutral. He was granted a few hours of peace each night when he was in his own cell.

Unfortunately, his quiet time was about to vanish. The inmates sharing Thornton's and Rea's cells were released after serving their jail time, and Thornton moved into Rea's cell as his new bunkmate. Now he was living with Thornton 24/7, and it was impossible to escape the man who talked constantly about using the act of murder to create a "partner bond," training little teenage girls, and having to commit murder in order to protect their pack. It was all too much for Rea. He felt as if he couldn't spend another moment with Thornton.

Rea felt as if his life had sunk as far down as he could go when he landed in jail. He went to the jail's chapel regularly to reflect on his life and examine the choices he had made. While being in custody was no picnic, Rea welcomed the routine, the opportunity to be far from drugs, and plenty of time for self-scrutiny.

Instead, Rea found himself looking back on his life and wondering what on earth he had done to deserve getting locked up with a violent psychopath like Thornton. Was something wrong with him? Of all the inmates in the county jail, why did Thornton choose to divulge his repugnant, evil deeds to Rea? Now that Rea shared a cell with Thornton, he never had a moment of peace. His only time alone was the rare occasion when Thornton had a court appearance or when Thornton was writing letters or working on his defense manifesto. Rea sought refuge in the chapel for prayer, but Thornton followed him there, too.

Perhaps, Rea thought, this was punishment, a test from God. He wanted to get away from this man, away from hearing about these horrific acts. Rea labored to keep his guard up. He couldn't let Thornton see him in a moment

of weakness, and he couldn't think about what would
happen to him if Thornton discovered Rea's secret and
turned against him.

Las Vegas, Nevada
April 4, 2001, 12:33 p.m.

"We need towels, darlin'. Room 104."

The dark-haired, middle-aged man stood at the front
desk of the Best Western Inn, fidgeting and foul with cigarettes.

"You're not getting any towels," clerk Phyllis Maynes
said flatly. She had already made her rounds of phone
calls at checkout time and Room 104, a mini-suite, hadn't
paid for another day and was checking out.

"You are not going to get service," Maynes said firmly
as she noticed the man becoming agitated. "You are
checking out, and I am not going to give you towels now."

"I paid my goddamned money, and I want towels!" he
blustered. "What's your problem? It's just goddammed
towels, for Chrissake!"

He was loud and upset, but Maynes stood her ground.
In her seventeen years as a clerk at a motel in Las Vegas,
there wasn't much she hadn't seen.

"If you want to stay over, you want to pay for tonight,
you will get service and you will get towels," she responded evenly. "You don't get maid service when you're
already a half-hour late for checkout."

He blustered a bit, but Maynes started ringing up his
bill anyway. The Best Western Inn was far from the Strip,
in the suburbs. A family-style Italian restaurant was next
door. An empty dirt lot sat across the street and a state
government building was down the highway. If they
wanted to experience the faded glory that had lured the
first tourists to the desert gambling oasis decades before,
the aging casinos of old Las Vegas were five blocks away.
To get to the edge of the main Strip, they would have to

go another two and a half miles south. Rooms at the discount motel were $54 per night.

"How many in the room?" she asked.

"Two," he answered.

Maynes glanced outside the large picture window and saw two teenagers standing on the sidewalk, talking outside the door to Room 104.

"Well, there were more than two in that room," she said. "Now are you checking out or what?"

"Keep your towels. I'm checking out," Thornton said, giving in. He dug into his wallet for a credit card, and Maynes looked at the kids standing there, waiting to leave. What did he want towels for anyway when his kids were waiting to leave, she thought. Kids under twelve were free, but these girls looked maybe fifteen or sixteen. Phyllis prepared his bill, entering "four" as the number of people in his room, a mini-suite. Guests often check into a motel and lie to the clerk about the number of people in the room, then sneak another half-dozen people in. That's why she drew a hard line on the towels. Maynes assumed the girls were his daughters and that his wife was also in the room, though she hadn't seen her.

They had checked in on April 2 at 11:54 a.m. and left April 4 at 12:33 p.m. With their AAA discount, their total amounted to $124.02.

Maynes shook her head. She didn't know why people lied about the number of people in a room when the price was the same for a suite.

Rialto, California
February 13, 2000, 8 p.m.

"How old are you?"

"I'm fourteen." Maria Rivera was sitting in the backseat of the Jeep. Michael Thornton, who looked older than her father, was driving. Janeen Snyder, who had been introduced as "Chris," was in the front passenger seat.

"How long have you been with your boyfriend?" asked Snyder.

"Two and a half years," she said.

Maria had long dark hair and stood not quite five feet tall. Her parents and little brothers lived near her boyfriend's family at a modest mobile home park in the working-class city of Fontana, where she was a freshman at Bloomington High. Seth Torres, sixteen, was her first love, but her parents disapproved. Seth had seen her father with another woman.

Her father's affair had been the source of constant fights between her parents, traumatizing Maria and her little brothers. When her father was with the other woman, her mother was either angry and upset at home or off being consoled at a friend's house, leaving Maria to care for her little brothers. Maria and Seth were going to slip away to the Motel 6 down the street to provide Maria a respite from her parents' constant bickering and give themselves some alone time for Valentine's Day. It was a big plan for a fourteen-year-old whose adolescent desire was to draw her parents' attention away from their own problems and back to her, a good student who had never before run away from home.

The impulsive teenagers had hatched their getaway plot just that morning. Maria would walk down the street and meet Seth at the Motel 6 where they would spend just two days before she walked home again. Their plan was foiled, however, by a hard rain that had not let up by 4 p.m. Seth called Maria to let her know he had booked the room, but that instead of walking in the rain, his friends Mike and Janeen would pick her up and take her to the motel. She would look for a green Jeep later between 7 p.m. and 8 p.m.

Maria's father had already left the house to spend time with the other woman and her mother was being consoled at a friend's house when Maria saw the Jeep pull up across the street from her house. Maria had planned to leave without telling her parents and would face the consequences after she got back in two days. At 7:30 p.m., Maria slipped quietly from the house carrying two shirts and two pairs of undies in her backpack.

Snyder was very nice to Maria and started asking her questions as soon as she got into the backseat. Thornton, who was driving, pulled up to the Albertson's grocery store in Rialto while Snyder continued to chat up Maria. She felt a little shy because she didn't know them, and she didn't know why they had passed the turnoff to the motel and why they were going to a grocery store. Maria had never ventured beyond the immediate neighborhood of her trailer park and high school, and she couldn't see clearly through the darkly tinted windows from the backseat of the Jeep on a stormy night. They had been driving for about twenty minutes, and she didn't know where they were. Snyder reassured her that they would pick up Seth at their house.

Snyder continued to ask Maria questions about herself, which Maria politely answered. Thornton didn't talk much. They walked the aisles and picked up armfuls of junk food—cake and Cheetos. They also bought Maria some nail polish and makeup. When they left the store, it seemed as if they were driving for a long time, but Maria was appeased by applying nail polish and using the makeup in the back seat. Before long, Thornton pulled up to a house on a dead-end street with a weedy, overgrown lawn. Maria was happy to see that Seth was there waiting for her. It was still raining hard and Seth told her that he wanted to stay there, but Maria didn't. Snyder finally talked Maria into staying, and she and Seth slept on an air mattress covered with a sheet on the floor. Instead of a door, strings of beads hung down from the door jamb. She found the house cluttered and dirty and she wanted to sleep on a real bed. She didn't know Thornton and Snyder. This was not Maria's idea of having some peace away from home.

The next morning, she asked Seth to take her home, but he ignored her and spent the day hanging out with Thornton and Snyder, smoking the weed they provided. She asked Seth again to take her home. When he didn't respond, she asked Snyder.

"Why do you want to go home for?" Snyder replied. She picked up a camera and took a picture of Maria with Seth. Maria didn't want to stay there anymore. She and Seth spent two days hanging around the house, primarily in the master bedroom that had been converted into a mini-theater. It had no bed, just an array of recliners facing a big-screen TV.

Thornton and Snyder seemed to have an endless supply of drugs. The couple was smoking something white out of a pipe more than ten times a day, and they provided Seth with marijuana. Maria had never used drugs and declined their offers to sample from a buffet of drugs they had lined up on a silver tray. For the second night in a row, Seth and Maria retired to the air mattress on the floor behind the bead curtain.

When Maria awoke the next morning, Seth was gone. It was the day she had planned to return home after their adventure. The youngster was getting homesick and thought that her mom would be worried about her. She wanted to go home. Maria didn't even know what city she was in.

She went from room to room looking for Seth, but instead found Thornton and Snyder in the master bedroom in their respective recliners, watching television and smoking the white powder in a pipe.

"I want to go home now," Maria said to Snyder.

"Why do you want to go home?" Snyder asked.

"I'm getting homesick," Maria said.

"OK," Snyder said as she resumed smoking. "I'll take you later. I promise."

Satisfied that she was going home, Maria folded her two shirts and her underpants in her backpack and waited. A few minutes went by, then an hour. She went back into the room and found Snyder and Thornton in the same recliners, still smoking. Maria again asked to go home and Snyder again reassured her. Snyder said that she would take her home, so Maria sat obediently and waited. On the fourth and fifth attempts, Maria had been asking more frequently until she was coming into the room every few minutes asking Snyder to take her home.

It didn't occur to Maria to hunt around the house for a phone, to walk out of the house to knock on a neighbor's door, or to find a gas station, because Snyder kept promising to take her home. Maria believed that she would. By evening, Maria was asking Snyder to take her home every few minutes, but Snyder challenged her.

"Why do you want to go home?" Snyder said. "You shouldn't go home," she said. She made sexual advances to the young teenager, suggesting that she and Thornton wanted her to be their girlfriend in the same way that she was Seth's girlfriend. Snyder offered Maria drugs from the silver tray, but Maria refused. Maria spent the third night curled up on the air mattress alone, terrified and unprotected behind the flimsy curtain of hanging beads.

As one day turned to the next, Maria asked to go home every few minutes. In reply, Snyder made graphic, sexual suggestions to her. Maria was desperate but realized that she was unable to escape without tripping a house alarm that sounded when a door or window to the outside was opened. Only one window stood ajar, and that was the small ventilation window in the bathroom adjoining the master bedroom. Maria waited until Thornton and Snyder were smoking in the master bedroom to enter the bathroom, thinking that she was small enough to climb out of the window. She stood on top of the toilet seat and tried to get through but got stuck through the window frame. With her head and left shoulder inside, standing tiptoe on the toilet seat, she wriggled helplessly, unable to move. A few minutes later, she heard the door open.

"What are you doing?" Snyder shouted.

Snyder reached up for her long, dark hair that hung past her shoulders and yanked hard, pulling her out of the window, then shoved her to the floor. To the young girl cowering on the floor, Snyder looked older, bigger, more physically powerful, and intimidating. Snyder turned on her heel and left Maria lying on the tiled floor. Too frightened to speak, Maria remained silent.

"You are not free to leave," Snyder said coldly. "It's written down in stone that you belong to us. We own you."

Maria stood before them, a prisoner. Or was she their slave? Confused and exhausted, Maria thought Seth had sold her to them.

There were rules. She had to be within arm's distance of either one of them at all times. If they were seated in their recliners, she was required to sit next to them on the floor. If she walked out of the room, she would "get in trouble" and would be punished. She was not permitted in any other area of the house besides the master bedroom or the second bedroom. She was required to follow around either Snyder or Thornton like a pet. Thornton told Maria that she was also required to perform sexual acts with both of them. She would sleep wherever Snyder wanted her to sleep. She wore clothes that Snyder wanted her to wear. Snyder took Maria's earrings, bracelet, and necklace. Stripped of her clothing and jewelry and robbed of her freedom, Thornton and Snyder were attempting to erase Maria's identity.

Days and nights passed with Thornton and Snyder smoking methamphetamine every half-hour in the master bedroom. Maria saw Snyder sleep only once and never saw Thornton asleep. They continued to push drugs on their victim. She continued to refuse them but obeyed the rules by following Snyder from room to room. In the kitchen, Maria stood within arm's reach, as required, as Snyder was cooking food.

"Don't leave," Snyder told her.

Maria obeyed and stood still, but Snyder unexpectedly took the spoon she had been using and pushed it against Maria's neck, holding it so long that Maria could hear the sickening noise of her sizzling skin. The burn branded Maria as theirs. She received no ice, no bandage, and no treatment for her burn. Snyder walked back into the master bedroom and Thornton, seated in a recliner, caught her eye. He pulled open the pouch on the side of the recliner so that she could see the gun he kept there. Then Snyder pulled open the pouch on the side of her recliner and showed her the gun that she had. In the kitchen, a shotgun stood next to the refrigerator.

Each day, Maria did as she was told and followed Snyder around the house. If she didn't, Thornton beat her and yelled at her, sometimes while holding a gun to her head. The youngster continued, at the point of a gun, to refuse performing sexual favors for either of them. They continued to harangue her, saying that she would "like it." As if arguing would convince her, Thornton explained that Snyder had engaged in sexual conduct with Thornton and his wife, Pamela, when Snyder was the same age as Maria.

"Oh c'mon, don't be like that, that's f-ed up," said an infuriated Thornton, delivering the remarks with his fists. "You're a bitch. You're the only one who won't give it up to me. What's up with that?"

At the point of a gun, Maria kept refusing. She could not recall how many times Thornton and Snyder had pointed a gun at her and beat her. On top of the physical bullying, Thornton intensified the psychological intimidation by sharing with Maria how they had become experts at molesting children and were too smart to get caught. He outlined his strategy: They changed cars with every victim. They took their young victims out in public in order to undermine the child's story that they were held captive. They made their victim write them a thank-you note.

"The way you get away with it is that you make the kid look bad," Thornton said. "You make 'em look like liars.

"You aren't the first, and you won't be the last," he told Maria, reaching for a set of Polaroid photos from a filing cabinet in the second bedroom with the bead curtain.

"*This* is what we do for a living," Thornton said, laying a half-dozen photos in front of her. "We molest kids," adding that they find young children and then train them to kill.

Maria was shocked by the photos, which showed Thornton and Snyder unclothed and engaging in sexual conduct with boys and girls that Maria estimated to be about the same age as her little brothers, from seven to nine years old.

Thornton bragged to Maria about killing people and gave her details. He told her about a man who had tried to rape Snyder. They bound him and Snyder performed a strip show for him. Thornton mutilated his genitalia and killed him. Thornton bragged about being a "hit man," but Maria didn't understand what that meant. Thornton was happy to explain that it meant that they were paid to kill people.

"You're the only one to resist us," Thornton said, beating her. "I hate you, you know that? I hate you 'cause you don't ever do shit. You're the only one that acts stupid since all the other girls and boys I have, they do everything I tell them to. You're the only one that's—has balls to actually deny and to actually say no to us."

"We're wolves," Snyder said. "You're the sheep."

They said that a lot but never explained to Maria what it meant. Even though she didn't know exactly why they kept talking about wolves and sheep, she knew that it was intended to intimidate her as much as everything else they told her.

The flood of information, the shock of being taken from her home and stripped of everything—her environment, her clothes, her earrings, her freedom—was terrifying to her, but she continued to resist.

"We've told you too much already," Thornton said. "If

you leave the house, you'll have to be dead. You'll be in a box."

Maria was becoming numb to the threats. She thought she was dead anyway. They had already told her that no matter what, she was never going to leave. If they were going to kill her, she would go somewhere better and she wouldn't have to put up with them anymore.

Snyder had been pushing Maria to engage in sexual activity and the next time Maria was in the shower, she joined her. Thornton and Snyder exposed Maria to X-rated films, and they engaged in sexual conduct in her presence and encouraged her to join in. Soon afterward, Maria woke up one morning feeling sick to her stomach. Her body was aching. She was surprised to see that she was in between Thornton and Snyder, who were nude, and that she was also unclothed. Thornton joked to her that he had molested her the night before, but Maria had no memory of it and couldn't recall going to bed at all the night before. The last thing she recalled was eating a cupcake.

Snyder, laughing, said that they had drugged her treat. Maria had suspected that they were drugging her food, because it hadn't tasted right. She had been losing her appetite and had been finding it hard to sleep. Though Snyder volunteered that they had been drugging her food, she didn't say how long they had been doing it. Before long, Maria felt a change in her body. She began to crave the drugs and started using them on her own. Like Thornton and Snyder, Maria began using meth every half hour. When she took drugs, she tended not to care about anything. Her body needed them, and that's all she cared about. When she was high, she got along very well with Thornton and Snyder. She didn't think about anything. Her brain went blank.

Sometimes she saw other people hanging out at the house, including a guy named Bobby. Once she went to him for help in trying to get away, but he told her, "That's your problem." Because they were friends with Thornton and Snyder, she didn't think they would be inclined to help her. She was afraid that they would hurt her, too, if she asked for help. When the couple's friends were at the house, they made no attempt to talk to Maria or get to know her—unless they wanted sexual favors. One friend tried to touch Maria. She pushed him away, and he told her to "quit fighting it." Snyder came into the room and slapped Maria for not letting him complete the assault.

The next day, Thornton put a piece of paper in front of Maria and pulled out his gun. He dictated and, with a gun to her head, she started writing:

"Mike, I really appreciate you letting me stay here," Maria, wrote. "I really appreciate what I have been able to do here. You are a really nice guy.

"Because I get treated with respect," she wrote. "I don't get treated like shit. Both of you understand me really good. You don't force me to do things. I get to learn a lot of things. Also, you both are nice and don't suddenly flip and hit me for saying something wrong.

"I'll try my very best . . . on doing my job right," she wrote. "Also, don't let anyone get to you. Just ignore them. Take care and stay in touch with me.

"Love always, Maria."

Maria wrote a second note addressed to Snyder:

"The first time I met you I thought you were awesome," it read. "The first two things I noticed from you was your beauty and your eyes. You have a very special gift. Protect it. Don't let anyone take it away. People would die to have it.

"Take very good care. Also, don't let anyone put you down.

"Love always, Maria."

Maria bore no recollection of writing either note, nor did she recall the instances when she was unable to fight off their sexual assaults. Thornton and Snyder supplied Maria with an unending stream of drugs every hour: methamphetamine to keep her alert, marijuana to keep her relaxed, and a combination of ecstasy and cocaine, making her a pliant and, at times, unconscious victim.

Days rolled into weeks while their teenage prisoner sat within arm's reach as they busied themselves with the busywork of "tweakers," or regular meth users: Thornton worked on his computer and Snyder did beadwork, or they watched movies. Sometimes they made movies of their own by using a video camera to record her refusing their sexual requests or her weeping after the assault when they overpowered her. They taunted Maria and laughed at her when they screened their home movies.

Scared and sick from being fed more drugs than food, Maria knew Thornton and Snyder mocked her to force her to act the way they wanted. She felt dirty after watching the X-rated movies, from being forced to watch Thornton and Snyder engage in sexual activities, and from their assaults. While Thornton and Snyder were tweaking, she had little to do but play with a few beads Snyder gave her, or entertain herself with a sheet of paper doodling Seth's name, over and over. She gazed out the window to the street hour after hour, digging her fingernails into her own skin. When it bled and formed scabs, she pulled them away.

Through dulled eyes, she thought she saw her father slowly drive by the house in his car, scanning the street looking for her. Frozen with fear and paralyzed by drugs, Maria could not move and was unable to discern reality from the rescue for which she desperately longed. Had she really seen her father? Was anyone looking for her? When would she see her family again? Would Thornton and Snyder ever let her leave?

Ten

Rialto, California
March 2000

"Look at her," Thornton bragged. He held court in the master bedroom, waving his methamphetamine pipe at Snyder in the chair next to his as he coldly discussed how he had deliberately manipulated her. Maria sat on the floor at their feet.

"I got her to do what I wanted because I molded her from a very young age," Thornton explained to Robert Thirkill, nineteen, another of Bobby Munoz's methamphetamine customers who had come to the house on Silver Circle Street for drugs but couldn't find a reason to leave. As the weeks turned to months, Thornton showed Thirkill his guns and shared his philosophy about mind control in the same matter-of-fact tone in which one would give advice about choosing a long-distance phone plan. Sometimes Thornton showed off his arsenal of weapons to Thirkill while they smoked methamphetamine and talked about girls.

"That's the way you do it with young girls, you get them

at a certain age, then you can, like, train them to be the way you want them to be," Thornton said. "Around the age of fifteen or so."

He had Snyder brainwashed. She would do what he wanted, Thornton said. His ultimate fantasy was "to find a girl of fourteen or fifteen, mold her, blend [*sic*] her, control her, manipulate her," and then kill her. Thirkill didn't take Thornton seriously and thought the worst he could do was swagger around the house waving guns around like "Billy bad ass." As the master of the house, Thornton wielded the law unto himself within his four walls. Thirkill had seen the young girl that Thornton kept in the back bedroom, like one kept a toy. He offered the girl to Thirkill, ordered her to comply, and left them alone. When the girl pushed him away a few minutes later, Snyder entered the room.

"Quit fighting!" she said. Snyder slapped Maria's face and turned on her heel, leaving her crumpled on the ground, crying. Thirkill and Snyder left the room, and Thornton offered Snyder to him as a substitute. Thornton returned to his computer where he was reviewing documents he had downloaded regarding the mind-control techniques of various groups, including psychologists, the U.S. military, and communist regimes. He also reviewed an online resource used by state and federal police, "Missing and Abducted Children: A Law Enforcement Guide to Case Investigation and Program Management."

Sierra Mobile Estates
Fontana, California
March 28, 2000

"Where's my daughter?" Lupe Rivera demanded.

With a slap to the face followed by a hard shove, Maria Rivera's mother body-slammed Seth's mother to the pavement, then jumped on the woman and pummeled her with both fists. The two women rolled around the parking lot of the mobile home park in a frenzy of punching and hair-pulling. While Lupe worked over Seth's mother, her husband Jorge and the half-dozen "homeboys" he brought with him tackled Seth and Seth's father. The parking lot brawl soon attracted the Fontana Police Department, landing Jorge in jail, but he didn't mind. Seth got the message.

It had been weeks since Maria disappeared and Jorge had either visited the police department or phoned every day since then, but he couldn't get anyone to take a report. The police told them that Maria was a runaway and would come home when she felt like it. Jorge, the manager at a local budget motel, knew that if he made more money or lived in a nicer part of town, the police would take him seriously. So Jorge and Lupe took matters into their own hands. Jorge convinced a local print shop to make 10,000 copies of a flyer he had made on his home computer. Jorge and Lupe began following Seth in the family van, hoping he would lead them to where Maria was being kept. Shortly after that, someone fired a shot at their house. Then someone smashed the windows of Jorge's car and slashed his tires. Their family van was stolen, and police found it destroyed. Despite the theft and the vandalism, Jorge and Lupe never stopped looking for their daughter. The couple received phone calls from a man and woman whose voices they didn't recognize threatening to burn them and their children alive in their mobile home.

When neighbors in the trailer park told them that Seth had bragged that he knew Maria's whereabouts, Jorge and his wife rounded up a few of their friends and confronted Seth and his parents. After the parking lot dust-up, Jorge was in jail for about a week.

A few days after Jorge's release from jail, Maria wobbled up the driveway, thin and preternaturally pale. Weak from lack of food and lack of sleep, she had blue and purple bruises covering her body and dark circles under her eyes. It had been days since she'd eaten. When she spoke, she spit up foam.

Lupe and Jorge rushed their daughter to the hospital, and the next day, over Maria's objections, they went to the police. Maria was willing to tell them what had happened to her, but when she began to relate her story, the male detectives laughed at her. Because she initially went to Thornton's house willingly, the detectives made her feel as though she were somehow responsible for what they did to her. Maria was terrified of Thornton and Snyder and had not recovered from weeks of being fed drugs instead of food. She exhibited textbook behavior of a sexual assault victim and, still essentially a child, was embarrassed to tell two grown men details of the numerous sexual assaults. Though she told them the rudiments of her six weeks with Thornton and Snyder, she was unable to divulge many of the details. The detectives told Maria and her parents that they would "look into it," but they did not take her to a hospital for the purposes of collecting evidence for a rape kit. They did not take photos of her multiple bruises, nor the prominent burn mark branding her neck.

Despite being force-fed drugs, the lack of food, the beatings, the repeated sexual assaults, and the humiliation of being treated like someone's pet, Maria had never stopped asking to go home. When she started to shake uncontrollably and foam at the mouth, Thornton thought she was overdosing.

"I don't want her to die at my house," he told Snyder as Maria sat inches away. Maria thought she was going to die anyway.

"You know what," Snyder said, looking over at Maria. "Let's go drop her off. I'm tired of this shit."

"All right," Thornton said. He reached down to where Maria was sitting, wrapped his hands around her throat and lifted her up off the floor, shoving her against the wall.

"If you go to the police, I will track you down, tie you up, glue your eyes open and make you watch us kill your family, starting with your little brother," Thornton said.

"If you leave the state, I'll kill 'em all, skin 'em, cut 'em up into little pieces, and send 'em to you piece by piece."

Snyder pulled her gun out of the pouch at the side of the recliner and used the barrel to push aside the waistband of Maria's pants.

"If you tell," Snyder said, moving the barrel of the gun downward under her clothing so that it touched her private area, "you die."

**Robert Presley Detention Center
Riverside, California
January 2003**

"As they sat together in the car, they realized it was their destiny to have met each other," Thornton wrote. "To MT, MC was the answer to a prayer . . ."

Jason Rea read through the pages Thornton handed to him describing the car trip he and Janeen Snyder had taken with Michelle Curran. After picking up Michelle in Las Vegas, they drove for hours to Thornton's home on the waterfront of Lake Arrowhead, which Thornton claimed had been burglarized by Tracy, his drug buddy, and the fictional Orlando. Rea continued reading Thornton's narrative, in which he used the third person and initials instead of their names: MT for Michael Thornton, JS for Janeen Snyder, and MC for Michelle Curran.

"The idea of running a salon in Las Vegas under MC's name seemed a Golden Opportunity. As for MC she was a joy to watch being so excited [about running a beauty salon]."

That part was true, Thornton said. He and Snyder had everything planned out in advance, and he had routinely floated the idea of running one of his salons as a ploy to each of their victims.

"We used it on Michelle," Thornton said of the insincere offer. "We did the same things on the other girl. That was before we picked up Michelle."

Once they reached the house at Lake Arrowhead, they spent the night at a nice resort a couple of miles down the road, then left for Mesa, Arizona, to stay at the house where Thornton's mother's lived because she was out of town. During the long trip to Arizona, Thornton wrote, "a lot of flirting took place." When they got to Mesa, to Thornton's surprise, both girls went into the shower and came out of the bathroom, unclothed and "dripping water."

In Thornton's depiction, he was the passive recipient of sexual attentions from a young woman and a teenager, but he told Rea that was a fabrication. Thornton and Snyder had put drugs in Michelle's food at an earlier point than when they had started feeding drugs to Maria. The first dose to Michelle was a "substantial" amount of methamphetamine, which Thornton deemed "very effective" because the mind-altering effect of the drug had reduced her inhibitions and allowed him to control her. Thornton created a powerful secondary level of control by intentionally getting Michelle addicted. She needed the drug, and she needed Thornton to supply it. To get drugs, she had to do what Thornton told her to do. Thornton said that he and Snyder also had used this tactic as well as the "good cop/bad cop" strategy on Maria, but Thornton did not mention Maria's name. Thornton's letter did not discuss the use of drugs or a gun as tools to control and intimidate Michelle. He also left out the fact that he took photos of Michelle unclothed.

"MT did mention to MC the 'I hope I get kidnapped' comments she had made and asked that before anything took place that she please write some kind of note to make sure that no one got the wrong idea about all them being together," Thornton wrote. According to his account, they were all "consenting adults" in a "voluntary and friendly relationship" who "preferred to be undressed" whenever they were alone.

"They had already told MC the story of their being falsley [*sic*] accused because some girl in California had lied to the police about them to protect her boyfriend," Thornton wrote.

"The 'I hope I get kidnapped' comment that MC had made became an ongoing joke between them." Rea had been unaware of the remarks Michelle had made as she stormed out her front door until Thornton told him. He found it fascinating that Thornton ruthlessly twisted Michelle's heartbreaking, final words to her family to force her to write him a make-believe legal protection to sexually assault her. In reality, Michelle wrote the note at the point of Thornton's gun.

"I told her what to write and she wrote the letter," he told Rea.

The sexual conduct also came at the point of a gun, Thornton told Rea. He had wanted to correct his mistakes from their prior victim and refine the conditioning process by forcing sexual contact earlier on. He had started by placing bindings on her that were light enough to escape to create a false sense of security that nothing would happen to her. He had bragged to Rea that he had acclimated Michelle to accept progressively restrictive bindings while giving her the feeling that she had control and establishing her trust. The ultimate goal was for the victim to be compliant. He did not want her to resist or fight when he took complete control over her at the moment they ultimately decided to take her life.

Sex with death was the ultimate goal.

Behind bars, Thornton continued his attempts to control Snyder long-distance via letter. He continued to express his love and affection for her to keep her pliable and willing to do what he wanted. He kept her close so she wouldn't divulge any information about their case. Rea knew that Thornton also wanted to control him.

Rea was frightened by what Thornton was telling him and knew that he had to watch his back. He didn't want Thornton to know that anything had changed about what he was feeling or what he thought about him as a person. Toward the end of January, Rea decided to reveal what Thornton had told him to the district attorney's office. The next time Rea went to court, he planned to tell his defense attorney that he had information for the DA. He couldn't risk being overheard in jail. He had to protect himself. If he became a snitch, an inmate who provided information to the prosecution or testified against a fellow inmate, and word got out around county jail, he would become a target. A snitch behind bars was guaranteed to be attacked or killed.

As Rea continued collecting details about Thornton's crimes, the irony was not lost on him that the very nature of Thornton's crimes involved living side-by-side with his victims in the close quarters night and day while keeping his true intent a secret. Thornton would have no idea that the tables had turned. Rea was very good at keeping a straight face.

Rialto, California
September 2000

To the United States Postal Service, Silver Circle was part of the city of Rialto, but it was in fact an unincorporated area. Any crimes that occurred in an unincorporated county area outside city limits fell under the jurisdiction of the San Bernardino Sheriff's Department. Three over-worked detectives were assigned by the San Bernardino Sheriff's Department to work general crimes in these unincorporated county areas, all of which were considered high crime zones. With one detective injured, two detectives remained to work general crimes investigations, a catch-all category for sex crimes, robberies, burglaries, assaults, all manner of drug violations, larceny and petty theft. San Bernardino Sheriff's Department detectives Debra Bauman and Sebastian Barnes served a search warrant at the house on Silver Circle on April 21, 2000, nearly a month after interviewing Maria. They arrested Thornton and Snyder, who spent a few hours behind bars before they remitted bail and were processed and released. During the search, detectives seized a handful of firearms and rifles, several holsters, multiple varieties of knives, handcuffs, duct tape, gloves, a Taser-style electric stun device, and two computers. None of this evidence was examined.

Maria's case was not investigated as the detectives rushed from case to case, "putting out fires," as Detective Bauman put it. Since there was never an investigation, no charges were ever filed, and Thornton and Snyder were never prosecuted for any crimes against Maria.

True to form, they ditched the green Jeep and used the light brown Suburban with Arizona plates that belonged to Thornton's mother. By the time they got their property back from the sheriff's department, they had moved from the Silver Street house to the cabin in Running Springs.

In September 2000, Thornton and Snyder celebrated Snyder's twenty-first birthday with a newfound declaration of their commitment to each other.

Thornton wrote a page-long letter on his computer to Snyder that he titled, "Partners."

So To My Love Who Turns 21
Today . . . goes All the Love &
Hate, Good & Evil, compassion
& savagery that my Heart can
beat into reality but loudest is
the beat of my Love for
My partner!!!

Michael

Eleven

Elizabeth Holt, fifteen, cautiously dipped her toe in the gurgling, steaming water. Her new friends had treated her to dinner, and they were partying at a fancy hotel suite with an in-room hot tub. It was cold outside, and Elizabeth gratefully settled into the hot water next to her new friends, Michael Thornton and Janeen Snyder, who was introduced to her as "Chris." Elizabeth was content with the first real meal she'd had in several days. Still high from the methamphetamine they had snorted after dinner, she was mesmerized watching strands of her long, red hair swirl in the water. The hotel was a few miles and a world away from the abusive household that Elizabeth had escaped and the dingy motel where she had met Thornton and Snyder. Elizabeth's mother was a methamphetamine addict, but instead of smoking or snorting the drug, she mainlined it with an IV. She was emotionally and physically abusive toward her daughter, and the state court had awarded legal custody of Elizabeth to her grandmother.

As a child, Elizabeth had bounced back and forth between her mother and grandmother, who couldn't accept the gravity of her daughter's drug problem or understand why Elizabeth strayed. At thirteen, Elizabeth had become a runaway, living in the alleys and dingy motels of downtown Riverside and sometimes in the homes of drug dealers who offered her a couch for the night. She had paired up with a street-wise drug user and sometime prostitute, Amanda Walker, nineteen, and the two redheads became "street sisters." Amanda looked out for Elizabeth and shared her food, found clothing, and lined up places for them to stay for a few days at a time. Every few months, the police or social services would sweep the streets rounding up runaways. Elizabeth would be returned to her grandmother only to find the streets again days later. Amanda had been introduced to Thornton and Snyder through a mutual drug contact and had learned that they had not one house but several, as well as the financial means to afford methamphetamine on a regular basis. To Amanda, Thornton and Snyder had seemed a friendly couple who could put up her street sister for a few nights. She'd told Thornton and Snyder that Elizabeth was a runaway who needed a place to stay because of an abusive, drug-addicted mother, and the couple agreed to meet her. Amanda brought them to Room 324 of the University Lodge in Downtown Riverside, a rundown motel popular with prostitutes and methamphetamine addicts where Amanda had arranged for Elizabeth to share a room with two of her drug buddies. When they knocked, a sleepy Elizabeth answered the door. Amanda introduced her to Thornton and Snyder, and they all casually sat and chatted cross-legged on the beds like college roommates.

"How old are you?" Thornton asked.

"Fifteen," Elizabeth replied.

Snyder took over from there.

"So, you're a runaway?" Snyder asked.

They talked for a while about Elizabeth's mother and her difficult childhood. Elizabeth liked Snyder, who did most of the talking and steered the conversation toward astrology, Tarot cards, and telling fortunes. She offered to tell Elizabeth's fortune and ran downstairs to grab her Tarot cards. She handed them to Elizabeth to shuffle three times, then set the cards down one at a time to predict her future. Snyder explained what the cards meant to Elizabeth, then exchanged looks with Thornton and they whispered to one another but didn't tell her what they were saying.

When they invited her to get some food, Elizabeth and Amanda agreed. Elizabeth left her meager belongings, clothing, and makeup in the room, expecting only to be gone overnight. They climbed into a motor home that Thornton maneuvered through a Kentucky Fried Chicken drive-through. After eating in the motor home, Thornton prepared lines of methamphetamine, which they snorted, then he drove to a very nice hotel near a fashionable mall in Riverside. After checking in, Amanda said she had to go to a party but would return soon, and she left Elizabeth alone with Thornton and Snyder.

Elizabeth felt happy with her new friends, but a little sad that Amanda had left without her. She pulled out her journal and jotted down some notes. Snyder asked what she was writing, and Elizabeth felt comfortable enough to share her thoughts.

"I wish I was surrounded by a bubble to keep everyone out," Elizabeth read aloud from her journal. The lonely teenager, abused and abandoned, talked about her essays and poetry on themes of isolation and depression. Submerged in the hot, steaming water, Thornton and Snyder reassured her that she wasn't the only one who felt that way. During the discussion of her journal entries, Thornton and Snyder exchanged knowing looks, indicating that they understood *exactly* what she sought to convey. Thornton told Elizabeth that both he and Snyder were a "certain kind of person."

"You are like us," Thornton told her.

To a fifteen-year-old runaway who was filled with

despair, anger, and the anguish of parental abandonment, Thornton and Snyder provided profound validation. Elizabeth believed they cared about her. She felt comforted to have finally found people who understood her. They talked for three or four hours, then the three curled up on the king-size bed, still in their street clothes, and fell asleep.

The next morning, Thornton and Snyder invited Elizabeth to stay at their house, and she agreed, thinking it was another one of the places Amanda had arranged for her to stay. On the drive to Lake Arrowhead, Snyder engaged her with questions about herself, her family, her feelings, and her writings, making her feel comfortable. When Snyder later invited herself into the bathtub with her, she didn't give it a second thought. They giggled and talked in the tub, their legs dangling over the edge. But a few days later, Elizabeth began thinking that things were not as they seemed with this couple.

The threesome was in the Jeep on their way to buy groceries when Thornton, who was driving, slowed down behind a young girl with shoulder-length brown hair, who wore a backpack. Thornton drove slowly behind her as she walked. From the backseat, Elizabeth looked out the window to see why they had slowed down. Thornton pointed to the girl up ahead and said that they were going to grab her, put her in the car, and then Elizabeth, who was in the backseat, would hold her down. Thornton seemed so intent on his prey, he didn't bother explaining to Elizabeth why they were going to put her in the car. He continued following the girl until she walked into a convenience store, and then Thornton drove away.

Later, as they shared methamphetamine at the house, Thornton casually told Elizabeth that they liked to rape and kill girls.

"I've killed thirteen people," Thornton said.

"I'm catching up," Snyder said.

A cold, hard fear gripped Elizabeth. Thornton and Snyder had invited her to stay at their house in Lake Arrowhead, and she had agreed but this was not like the other places to stay that Amanda had found for her. Inside their own house, Thornton and Snyder pulled guns out of their coats, boots and purse. Elizabeth counted the noses of five shotguns lined up by the front door. More guns and stacks of cash were stashed throughout the motor home, in cabinets and behind the television set. Snyder saw that Elizabeth was taken aback and redoubled her efforts to make her feel comfortable. They spent all day together talking, with Snyder asking her to share her deepest thoughts and talk about her writings.

Elizabeth realized she had been deceived. Thornton and Snyder were not the nice people that they had pretended to be. And she had noticed that she was the same age as their ideal targets. She vowed that she would not end up one of their prey.

In the days that followed, Thornton and Snyder hunted for girls whenever they left the house to buy food or drugs. The girls were usually walking home from school with backpacks or books, and they were always alone. They looked to be between thirteen and sixteen, with long hair and petite builds. Just like Elizabeth.

When they all returned home one evening, Snyder invited herself into the bathtub with Elizabeth, who hadn't given the behavior a second thought in their first days together. She now realized that they had never left her alone during the time she had been with them. Scared and feeling more alone than ever, Elizabeth decided that she had to leave; her life depended on it. Escaping from the house in Lake Arrowhead posed a steep hurdle to a young teenager who didn't know how to drive or even have access to a car. She knew she would have to wait for the right opportunity to escape. Until then, she told herself to go along with whatever they suggested and not disagree or argue.

When they got out of the bath, Thornton and Snyder saw that Elizabeth had grown quiet, but she tried not to let them know that their conversation about raping and killing girls had bothered her as much as it did. Thornton told her that Snyder used to come to his daughter's birth-day parties when she was twelve years old. After realizing that they had a "connection," Snyder would run away from home just to be with him. Snyder, like Elizabeth, also came from a troubled home. Eventually, Snyder convinced his daughter, who was the same age, to invite her to stay with her family. Thornton and Snyder tried to convince Elizabeth that her situation was a lot like Snyder's. Elizabeth tried to steer the conversation toward the writings in her journal and soon the three were rapt in conversation about how Elizabeth's mother had treated her.

As Elizabeth related episodes from her life, Thornton asked helpfully, "Do you want me to kill your mom for you?"

Elizabeth was stunned into silence. She sensed that Thornton was either trying to protect her or frighten her. Despite her family's problems, she didn't want her mother murdered.

"What's your mom's address?" Snyder asked.

Elizabeth lied and said that she didn't know.

The next night, Snyder asked Elizabeth to model suggestive, skimpy outfits, and they both paraded around the living room, showing them off for Thornton. A few days later, Elizabeth didn't object when Snyder asked if she wanted to play with hot wax by dripping the wax from lit candles on themselves. Before long, the couple asked her to join in their sexual activity. Elizabeth didn't want any part of it, but she knew it was a trade-off in order to stay alive. If she refused, she would be forced to do whatever they wanted her to do at gunpoint, and then be killed.

Elizabeth noticed that there were no phones at the house, and they carried cell phones in their pockets. During a quiet moment, Elizabeth asked if she could call her grandmother just to let her know that she was okay, but Thornton assured her that they would see her grandma as soon as they went back down the hill.

A few days later, after one of their baths, Thornton gave Elizabeth a robe. She put it on and tied the belt around her waist, even though Thornton and Snyder wore their robes around the house, untied, with nothing on underneath. For dessert that evening, Snyder brought out two bowls of rocky road ice cream from the kitchen. After Elizabeth had eaten about a third of the ice cream, Snyder told her that it was laced with magic mushrooms. Thornton did not eat any but sat on the chair watching them.

"It's going to feel good and be fun." Snyder told her, taking another bite.

Elizabeth had never had a hallucinogenic drug, and the girls giggled as they sat on the couch. Snyder and Elizabeth went outside and walked around and played in the snow where everything felt weird and cartoonish. When they came back inside, Thornton played some unusual music with hard-to-understand lyrics that he said pertained to wolves. Then he started talking to her about wolves.

"You looked like everyone else, but you are really a wolf in disguise," he said. "That's why you've been feeling the way you wrote about in your journal. You feel like you're different from everyone else, because you are different.

"You're a wolf," he said. "I am a wolf, and [Snyder] is a wolf, too." Thornton used the term "wolf" and "partner" interchangeably.

"So you are telling me I belong here?" Elizabeth asked, crying. The drug blunted her fear and she felt blissful and mellow.

Nobody understood her, Thornton said, because she was a wolf. But Thornton and Snyder understood. They were all wolves, or partners, and they were a pack. Each member of a wolf pack protects the other. Wolves, or partners, kill for one another.

"That's why we always have each others' backs," Thornton said.

Elizabeth was crying and emotional. She felt as if she belonged.

"What about the people who aren't wolves?" she asked.

"They're sheep."

"What is a sheep?"

"The people that wolves wanted to kill," Thornton said. "We kill the sheep."

Despite being under the influence of hallucinogenic mushrooms Elizabeth couldn't accept Thornton's remarks about raping and killing young girls.

"What if, what about children?" she asked. "You'd kill a child?"

"Yes," Thornton answered. "If they see your face, you have to kill them. We are the wolves, the other people are sheep, and the wolves kill the sheep."

Elizabeth felt a flood of tears. She was terrified and didn't understand "the whole wolf thing." She was whacked from the drugs, and Thornton and Snyder's evangelical fervor to convert her into a wolf and it was too much for her to handle. Thornton had underscored the duty of wolves to protect one another, but Elizabeth just wanted to get far, far away from these people.

Thornton told Elizabeth that he and Snyder had been arrested for kidnapping a girl, who they said had falsely accused them for enjoying the same kind of "relationship" they had with Elizabeth. They asked her to do something for them, for the pack. For her fellow wolves.

"We want you to kill her," Thornton said.

Elizabeth could not hide the terror on her face.

"She's scared, Mike," Snyder said. "I can see she's too scared to do it."

Elizabeth understood that she was being tested. They were serious. And they were careful. That prior arrest explained why Thornton hid a handcuff key on the inside of his belt.

"I'm not scared," Elizabeth said.

But she was scared. Elizabeth would never kill a child, but was terrified to outwardly disagree. She understood what they were doing and why they asked *her* to kill the girl in order to join their group. It was the girl's punishment for going to the police, but it was also intended to be an incentive for Elizabeth not to tell anyone what they were doing or the same thing could happen to her. If and when she escaped, Elizabeth resolved never to tell the police what Thornton and Snyder had done, because then they would pressure the new girl to kill her.

More than three weeks after Elizabeth joined their "pack," Thornton and Snyder took her on a road trip to pick up money and do a hit for Thornton's mother in Mesa, Arizona. Elizabeth understood that they not only liked killing people, but that was how they earned a living. On the long drive, Thornton and Snyder discussed their careers as "hit men," and Snyder amused herself by seeing how many words she could make out of the phrase "hit men rule." Many of the four- and five-letter words she came up with were misspelled or not universally recognized. She made crossword and word search puzzles from the ones she liked.

When they arrived at Thornton's mother's house in a retirement community, Thornton parked the motor home directly outside the window of Thornton and Snyder's bedroom and they left Elizabeth outside to sleep in the motor home. Alone for the first time in weeks, Elizabeth sat in the RV and weighed her options. She knew she couldn't just walk away without a plan. She immediately ruled out going to Thornton's mother for help. Given the couple's methamphetamine habits, there was no guarantee that they would sleep during the evening hours. If she slipped away from the motor home, it would only be a matter of moments before they started shooting at her. And where would she run to in a retirement community? It didn't matter, because that window of opportunity slammed shut after just one evening. The next day, they got on the road back to California with bundles of cash that Elizabeth estimated to be more than $2,000.

In the middle of the desert, miles from any speck of civilization, Thornton unexpectedly turned off the highway, drove for a while in the desert, and parked. There was not a single person around, not a car, not a building, nothing. Thornton picked up one of his guns and asked Elizabeth to step outside the motor home. Her knees were shaking as she stood outside. Thornton fiddled with his gun.

"We like to take people out to the middle of nowhere," Thornton said, "and kill them."

Elizabeth could scarcely breathe.

"I like to tie them to a rock, rape them, and shoot them," he said.

Thornton walked over to Elizabeth with his gun, handed it to her, and then taught her how to fire the weapon.

"Shoot at the ground," he ordered, stepping back. Elizabeth tried firing at the ground but couldn't get the gun to work. She looked back at Thornton and saw that he was pointing his gun directly at her. Snyder stood behind him.

Elizabeth froze.

"Why isn't this working?" she asked in a very small, scared voice.

Thornton took a sudden step toward her and took the safety off the gun. Elizabeth dutifully fired three rounds into the ground, and they all climbed back into the motor home. Her ears were ringing so badly she could barely hear. Before they reached the highway, Thornton paused and looked back at Elizabeth at the rear of the motor home.

"Are you surprised you made it out alive?" he asked, shooting her a vicious look. She had never before seen his face twisted into a nasty grin.

Elizabeth felt more like the sheep than the wolf they claimed she was. Nevertheless, when they returned, Thornton handed her a very small, silver .22-millimeter gun, the length of her wrist to her finger, and called her "partner." Thornton gave her the gun from time-to-time, then he would take it back. Elizabeth knew that Thornton and Snyder carried at least one or two guns on them, even inside the house. The tiny .22 was no match for the shotguns, rifles, the .38 Snyder carried in her purse, and the array of handguns wielded by two professional hit men. She had to be patient.

On their next drug-buying trip to Riverside, Thornton pulled the motor home into the familiar parking lot at the apartment building of Amanda Walker's sometime boyfriend. All three of them walked into his apartment and completed the drug transaction, then Thornton pulled Elizabeth aside to one of the bedrooms and handed her the little gun. He told her to lie down in the back closet to hide and wait for Amanda.

"When we see her, we'll come in and tell you," Thornton said. "Then you come out and shoot her."

Elizabeth stood dumbfounded, the small gun heavy in her hand.

"We want you to kill Amanda, because she left you with people like us," Thornton told her.

He opened the door to the closet and told her to lie down, which she did. Tortured logic aside, Elizabeth believed in the pit of her stomach that she really would have to shoot Amanda. She was petrified and didn't want to kill "street sister," but she was afraid to disagree. Surrounded by clothing, the teenager lay in the dark, tears rolling down her face. The reality was that she could never shoot Amanda and she was the one who was going to die, not Amanda. Once Thornton and Snyder saw that she could never pull the trigger, Elizabeth feared they would kill her because she could not fulfill her duties as a member of their wolf pack. And the penalty for that was death.

Elizabeth huddled for what seemed like hours in the closet. Thornton finally entered the room and opened the closet door to tell her that Amanda was a no-show. Emotionally drained, Elizabeth staggered to her feet and they escorted her to the motor home where Thornton asked for the gun. They all returned to Lake Arrowhead.

A few days later, Yvette Perkins, a friend of Thornton and Snyder's, showed up at the front door with a little

girl, Brittany, who was eight or nine years old and was
going to stay with them for a few days. During the day,
they all colored and played in the snow, giving Thornton
and Snyder a distraction and Elizabeth a much-needed
break. Perkins arrived a few days later to pick up her
daughter. Elizabeth was certain that Thornton and Snyder had assaulted the little girl, and she was troubled that
she couldn't prevent them from hurting her. When the
little girl left, Elizabeth was again alone with them, and
their unwanted sexual activity.

On their next trip down the hill to Riverside, Thornton
and Snyder purchased drugs and groceries and made the
round of their salons. Elizabeth never asked questions
about their personal business. When they pulled up to the
bank, Snyder told Elizabeth that Thornton laughed in a
particular way before he killed someone. She got out of
the car and Thornton, in the front seat, turned around and
gave Elizabeth, in the backseat, a very scary, maniacal
laugh. Though it had just been four weeks, it seemed like
years since Elizabeth had felt safe on the streets. Now
Thornton and Snyder were toying with her; perhaps they
were getting tired of her. Elizabeth sensed that they were
going to kill her soon. They drove to one of their hair
salons on their next stop, and Thornton worked on his
laptop in the back office while Snyder scooped cash out
of the safe. It was after hours, and Elizabeth wandered
around the empty salon, playing with the hair products.
When she passed by the office, she saw Thornton sitting
with his feet propped up on the desk.

"Let's kill Elizabeth," she heard him say. "I want to
shoot her and burn this place down."

She raced to the front of the salon and tried the door,
but it was locked from the inside. The other exit would
take her past the office to the rear of the salon. She picked
up a magazine in the reception area and thumbed through
it, staying close to the front windows that overlooked a
shopping area. Snyder came out of the office and asked
her to come over to one of the booths. Trembling, Eliza-

beth dropped the magazine. Snyder was looking at hair color and selected one for Elizabeth. It was a blond-red color called "Paprika." After Elizabeth's first hit, Snyder explained, she would need to change her appearance. Snyder pocketed the hair color, and the three returned to the motor home and headed back to Lake Arrowhead. On the way, they would pass within a short distance of the University Lodge where she had been staying when they first met. This could be her only chance.

Elizabeth, who rarely spoke up, asked if they could drop her off so that she could pick up the rest of her things. To her surprise, Thornton agreed. She held her breath and tried not to appear too anxious as he pulled up to a donut shop at the corner a half-block away. Thornton asked her to meet them there when she had collected her belongings. Alone for the first time since meeting Thornton and Snyder, she walked in the direction of the lodge, all the while keeping the motor home in the corner of her eye. As the vehicle slid out of sight into traffic, she ran as fast as she could past the sleazy motel, hiked the fence to the back alley, and half-ran, half-walked toward her grandmother's house miles away, looking over her shoulder every step of the way. She was well aware of the consequences of breaking from the pack. She knew that they would never have let her go. She knew too much. Elizabeth vowed never to tell the police or anybody where she had spent the past five weeks. At the earliest opportunity, Elizabeth left California for the East Coast and never looked back.

Riverside County District Attorney's Office
Riverside, California
February 6, 2003

Jason Rea brought proof.

Lots of upwardly mobile inmates get themselves housed with a high-profile inmate who is awaiting trial, read up on the details of a case, then claim that the inmate "confessed" to them. Most don't make it past the day duty investigator at the DA's office. Rea arrived at his appointment with district attorney investigator George Hudson carrying an accordion folder full of papers, including Thornton's fifty-seven-page letter and the names and addresses of witnesses—all in Thornton's handwriting. Hudson made copies of everything Rea brought with him. For the next three hours, Rea told Hudson everything he knew, unloading the horrific and disturbing details that Thornton had given him, which Rea had carried with him for months. But that was the easy part.

Hudson had to return Rea to his cell and talk to Thornton like nothing had happened—as if he hadn't spent the entire afternoon in the DA's office slamming the door shut on the prosecution's case and becoming a lynchpin in his death penalty murder trial.

If anyone were to find out that he was a snitch, Rea's life would be in jeopardy. Hudson arranged for the jail deputies to explain his absence with a cover story that he had been rebooked on an additional charge.

The rest was up to him.

Twelve

It was the last day of the Fontana Police Department Canine Pals Carnival when Maria Rivera's parents dropped her off there with her little brother. The small Ferris wheel, a carousel, a mini-roller coaster for little kids, and the carnival games, like toss-a-coin and get-a-goldfish, were close together on a small plot of the parking lot of a shopping complex with the Food 4 Less grocery store on one side and K-Mart on the other. They had been waiting in line for tickets less than ten minutes when a girl approached them.

"Are you Maria?" the girl asked. "Do you remember me?

"I'm Michelle."

Maria didn't recognize her. She was a white girl, really pretty and very tiny. She had long, dark, wavy hair and a small scar on the top of her lip. She wore black pants and a black sweater. She had details about Maria, where she went to school and people she knew.

"Come with me and my sister and my sister's boyfriend," she said. "We're getting something to eat."

"Um, no thanks," Maria Rivera said.

Michelle continued coaxing Maria to come with her.

"We have weed," Michelle said. "Do you want to smoke weed?"

"No, I got my little brother," Maria said.

"He can come too," Michelle said. "C'mon, just come with us! They're waiting."

After a few minutes, Michelle left and crossed the parking lot to talk to some people in a brown Suburban with tinted windows. She returned and again tried to convince Maria to go with her. She even wrote down her name and a pager number on the back of a carnival ride coupon.

It had been just over a year since Maria had been released by Thornton and Snyder. Home at last, she shook and cried in a way that her parents had never seen. Maria was so afraid to leave her house that she dropped out of high school. Her parents considered attending a police-run carnival on Easter Sunday to be a safe outing for Maria and her little brother.

For four hours, Michelle followed Maria and her brother around the small carnival, going back and forth between them and the Suburban, but Maria continued declining Michelle's invitations.

Finally, it was time to take her brother home.

"C'mon," Michelle said. "We'll take you home."

Maria refused. She was not leaving with anyone she didn't know.

Michelle returned to the Suburban empty-handed, and Thornton was livid. It was a failed mission. Neither he nor Snyder had told Michelle that they sought murderous revenge against Maria for reporting them to police. But allowing Michelle to wander alone for hours at a police carnival with money in her pocket and free access to responsible adults fulfilled another objective. She could have approached any carnival employee, any security guard, or any of the police officers at the carnival to ask for help, or simply disappeared into the crowd and walked away forever. Thornton had been certain that she would not do so. The weeks of programming had resulted in exercising complete control over Michelle. He knew she wouldn't run.

Thornton and Snyder's conditioning of Michelle, as well as the documentation of her apparent liberty, echoed that of previous victims and was nearing preparations for the final event—her death. Michelle's final days were spent with the proud couple trotting their trophy around to friends and drug buddies to serve their own purpose as evidence that she was a calm and willing companion. She was taken to his mother's house in Arizona and forced at gunpoint to write a note praising and thanking the couple for their hospitality. On the return trip, they taunted Michelle with a detour off a remote desert highway, as they had done with Elizabeth. The surprise tutorial in shooting a firearm served less as an educational opportunity and more as a lesson in intimidation, given Michelle's fear of guns.

They meticulously documented Michelle's purported cooperation with photos, audio tapes, and visits to their drug buddies. Although they intended to end Michelle's life soon, they hid the evidence in case they needed it—it was Michael's obsessive need to plan ahead. The letter Michelle penned at gunpoint was stashed in a cabinet at his mother's Arizona home. Photos of her being conditioned with various restraints were secreted in a backpack. Audio tapes were shelved under layers of debris in the Suburban. The act of documentation formed a two-tiered structure of domination and coercion. Each picture snapped of Michelle, each tape of casual conversation with her captors, and each social encounter with friends reinforced Michelle's helplessness to resist them and underscored the futility of reporting their untoward behavior to authorities, if she ever dared to.

Thornton had increased the frequency and doses of methamphetamine and marijuana so much that Michelle gagged from dehydration. She remained as compliant as a rag doll. He could take her out to a restaurant with friends, and when the server asked for her order, she paused, then answered obediently, "I'll have whatever Mike wants me to have."

It was no mistake that Thornton had booked a room at the Motel 6 in Fontana the night before the carnival, and that it was less than a block away from where the carnival was being held. One of his drug contacts had heard from a friend who sold drugs to Maria's parents that Maria was planning to be at the carnival that day. Michelle's days were numbered, and when she failed to pick up Maria, Thornton gave her one more chance.

Rubidoux, California
April 17, 2001, 11:45 p.m.

"Did you say Brittany's not there?" Thornton asked.

"So far, no," Snyder answered.

Thornton, Snyder, and Michelle were riding around in the Suburban looking for eight-year-old Brittany, who had visited Thornton and Snyder at their Lake Arrowhead home for a weekend in the snow a few months before. Thornton was angry with Brittany's mother, Yvette Perkins, because he believed that she had broken into their home and stolen cash and drugs. He wanted revenge against her by kidnapping Brittany and killing her in the same way they did Jessie Peters. To commemorate the event, Snyder had created a mixed work of collage and sketch art titled "Sorry, Yvette," featuring a hand wrapped around the throat of a little girl, choking her.

The night before the expedition to find Brittany, Thornton, Snyder, and Michelle had socialized with friends, including Daniel Davis, a fellow methamphetamine user.

Thornton showed Davis the rifle that he selected to use once he found Yvette and Brittany.

"I am going to use this to kill people," Thornton told Davis. "I'm gonna smoke 'em."

It wasn't the only weapon in the Suburban.

Two weeks before the trip to Las Vegas in which they had kidnapped Michelle, Thornton had asked Davis to procure "an untraceable gun." Davis found a .380 Colt pistol, brand-new in the box for five hundred dollars. He handed Thornton the gun, and Thornton gave him cash.

"Here you go, baby," Thornton said, handing Snyder the gun.

She replaced the semi-automatic she usually carried in her purse with the new pistol. Snyder's newest weapon was the same gun she had practiced shooting in the desert in front of Michelle.

The next day Thornton cruised the streets of Rubidoux with Snyder and Michelle, going up and down the street where Yvette lived. They stopped people on the street asking if they'd seen Yvette or Brittany. They waited outside the bus stop where Brittany would exit the bus and walk home. There was no sign of either of them. After several hours of driving around looking for them, they gave up. But all was not lost. Thornton hadn't only been looking for Brittany that day; he had been scouting for a place to stage Michelle's murder.

Thornton and Snyder were bored with Michelle. Like Maria, Michelle had been asking to go home. The teenager who walked around with a phone glued to her ear missed her friends. She missed her sister. She had left her new boyfriend, Steve, just as their relationship was starting to blossom. The fastidious and fashionable dresser who spent hours planning her wardrobe had worn the same outfit for two weeks straight. She was terrified of the couple and afraid to ask to go home, but it was a constant undercurrent. Though they had selected Michelle as a "kill" for Snyder, the young girl had started to grow on Thornton and Snyder was extremely unhappy about that.

Could it be possible that he would replace Snyder with Michelle? Was she about to become a "partner"? Was Michelle's presence a threat to Snyder's status in the "pack?"

On Easter Sunday night after the carnival, Thornton and Snyder took Michelle to visit Elena Broussard, a hair stylist at one of the salons, and her husband. They pulled up and parked the motor home in their driveway. Broussard gave Snyder a cut and color at her house, and Snyder vented heatedly about Thornton's preferential treatment of the "little bitch." She thought Thornton was doting on Michelle, doing things for her and getting her anything she wanted.

"I'm his girlfriend, not her," she spat, not caring whether Michelle was in earshot. " 'Michelle, do you want something to eat? Are you OK with that? Did you enjoy the food?' "

"Why is she getting special attention and not me?" Snyder said. "He's waiting on her hand and foot!"

Angry and upset, Snyder was starting to think that *she* was the third wheel in the relationship.

On Monday night, Thornton, Snyder, Michelle, and Daniel Davis went to Denny's for dinner, and Snyder's jealousy erupted at the table. Snyder left the restaurant to smoke a cigarette, and Davis followed her outside as she complained to him the way she had complained to Broussard. When Thornton joined them, Davis excused himself but overheard their angry words about how well Thornton was treating Michelle.

After a sleepless night, they packed their things early Tuesday morning to ready themselves to hunt for Chelsea. Loud yelling drew Broussard out of the house at 2:15 a.m., and she saw Thornton screaming at Snyder. A tearful Snyder fled into the house, and Thornton followed. They continued the fight inside in full view of Broussard, her husband, and a tiny Michelle curled up on the couch. Thornton apparently had had enough. He took a hard swing and struck Snyder in the chest and shoulder area.

"This is your last fuckup, or you're out of here," Thornton said as he dropped Snyder to the floor.

As they drove around town looking for Brittany, Snyder was particularly interested in locating the girl, since she thought that the girl would provide Thornton with a temporary distraction. When they could not locate her, perhaps Snyder believed that Thornton would find himself bored with Michelle instead of her.

"Do you like swimming, Michelle?" Thornton asked. "Maybe we can find a place to swim."

It was 1:45 p.m., and they had pulled up to the ranger's booth at the entrance to Rancho Jurupa State Park. It was three miles from their Motel 6, half a mile from Yvette and Brittany's house, and a half a mile from Brittany's school bus stop. After watching Thornton drown Jessie Peters, Snyder knew better than to get in the water, but she encouraged Michelle to go in.

"It's hot today," Snyder said. "Wouldn't it feel good to cool off?"

Thornton had taught her well. Snyder knew that going swimming was a pretext for making the victim comfortable. It was like taking a bath, the way she had offered to get in the bath with Jessie, with Maria, and with Elizabeth. The victim is caught off-guard and not suspecting harm to come in the bath or pool, and they're unclothed and helpless. Thornton wanted to get Michelle into some water so that she would be comfortable and he could kill her. When they drove out to the ponds, Thornton climbed in first, jeans and all, while Snyder stood on the bank, and Michelle did, too. No amount of convincing would lead her to climb into a stagnant pond with slimy, green algae. They all climbed back into the car, and Thornton quickly drove back to the Motel 6 to change into dry clothing.

Now Thornton was angry. He'd forgotten his favorite snub-nosed .38 revolver in the pocket of his Levi's. They got back into the car, and Thornton shoved a paper clip into the locking mechanism of the rear passenger door so it could only be opened from the outside and mumbled something about the door being broken.

On the search for Brittany earlier that day, Thornton had earmarked a couple of locations to stage the murder. The first possibility looked occupied, so they went to the second location, a secluded, isolated ranch with a couple of outbuildings and a locked gate. It even had a place to hide the car around the back so that you wouldn't see it from the street. Thus, it seemed a better choice. Yvette and Brittany Perkins's house was just three hundred yards from the ranch. They drove up to the gate, and Snyder saw a lock wrapped around it. Good news. The owner was gone. Thornton parked in the dirt driveway, fished the bolt cutters out of the back, and snapped off the lock, leaving the shiny, twisted piece of metal in the dirt.

Robert Presley Detention Center
Riverside, California
February 13, 2003

"Did you read it?" Thornton asked. "What did you think of the last few pages?"

Thornton had hurriedly written the conclusion of his letter explaining the turn of events from his standpoint and given the final pages to Rea to read and review. Though Rea had not seen the crime scene and wasn't sure what "tack" was, it sounded surreal. He had been extremely careful to remain expressionless and put on his game face in the final few days he had to spend behind bars with Thornton. The two had scarcely been apart since Rea had secretly met with Hudson. Despite the convenient story that Rea had been rebooked on additional charges, he was under extreme pressure as an active snitch who was still behind bars gathering information for the DA. He was placing his own life on the line for their case, and in exchange, he would not get a dime or a reduced sentence. It didn't matter to him. Thornton was a sick bastard.

At Hudson's request, corrections officials arranged for Rea to be moved to another pod for his own protection. It wasn't uncommon for jail authorities to move inmates around within an institution, and in preparation for Rea's move, Thornton redoubled his efforts to provide Rea with documents, addresses, and notes, and hastened completion of his letter. After being in custody for nearly two years, Thornton and Snyder had a trial date the following year and Thornton's compulsion for planning pushed him to hand Rea everything he had. After Rea was released and he delivered the material to Snyder's defense attorney, the attorney's investigator could prepare their defense for the trial.

To Rea, the letter read like a contrived fantasy letter in a men's sex magazine. Thornton claimed that once they arrived on the property, he was drawn, for some reason, to an open window overlooking the kitchen area and inexplicably grabbed a cup full of pens. He brought the cup of pens over to show the girls what he had found, as if there were something intrinsically fascinating about a cup of pens. By the time he turned around, he wrote, the girls had discovered the tack room and its array of leather straps, ropes, long cords, and leather crops. Thornton painted himself as a hapless bystander subject to the whims of two young, playful nymphomaniacs.

When Thornton met with Rea for the last time, they walked together in the day room and he explained how everything for which he had trained Michelle unfolded in the tack room. Planned by him, orchestrated by him, the murder ultimately happened on his command.

Thornton told Rea that he parked the Suburban out of sight behind the house so that he and Snyder could remove her shoes and pants and bind the terrified teenager's wrists and ankles with duct tape. Thornton ripped Michelle's spaghetti-strap shirt in half, leaving just half of it hanging from her body. It was Thornton who rigged the tack, then hoisted Michelle to suspend her mid-air. During the sexual assault, Snyder stood by with a loaded gun.

Thornton wanted Michelle's last memory to be of him sexually assaulting her. She resisted a little, which he didn't like. He thought that he had trained her better. His end game was to assert complete control over the victims. Thornton didn't want her to struggle or resist *at all*. Snyder, also conditioned not to resist Thornton, was responsible for monitoring Michelle, and she responded by cocking back the hammer of the gun. As soon as Michelle heard that, she stopped squirming.

Thornton told Rea that he was "very satisfied" knowing that the bound and gagged teenager would die at any moment. There came a point when Michelle understood that she would not be untied and that she was not going to get away. Thornton said that he liked the look on her face when she realized she was going to die.

As Thornton spoke, Rea saw what can only be described as a look of ecstasy on his face. Thornton simply glowed when he talked about looking at Michelle's face as he killed her. He ordered Snyder to shoot and she fired, using the untraceable gun he had purchased for her days before their trip to Las Vegas.

"Do you know what it's like to shoot someone while you're [sexually assaulting] them?" Thornton said. "The look on their face?"

As he spoke, his eyes flashed with excitement and, Rea noticed with disgust, Thornton drooled.

Within minutes, a deputy arrived to escort Rea to his cell to box up his few belongings. Hudson had arranged for Rea to be transferred to the Southwest jail in Temecula. Rea hoped that his game face masked the mix of revulsion and relief at finally being taken away from this monster. They shook hands, and he bid Thornton good-bye.

Rea couldn't walk away from him fast enough. He

wanted to be out of his sight, out of the pod, and as far away from him as possible. He was emotionally exhausted. He had beaten Thornton at his own game, surviving for months in custody, living side-by-side with a master of manipulation, learning excruciating details about Thornton's homicide case without divulging what he had successfully kept Thornton from learning about him. Thornton never knew that he had spilled his secrets to a gay male. If Thornton had reason to suspect that Rea was cooperating with the prosecution *and* that he was gay, Rea would not have lived long enough behind bars to walk away.

Instead of being moved to his new quarters, Rea was escorted into an interview room to meet with Hudson. With a rush of relief, he handed over the last documents that Thornton had given him. He spent hours telling Hudson everything Thornton had just revealed to him about Michelle's final moments in the tack room. Hudson said that Rea would be brought to court in another month for sentencing in his own criminal case and reiterated that he would not receive any special dispensation for his cooperation, which would prevent the defense from attacking his credibility as a witness.

Rea would serve the remainder of his several weeks of his sentence in Temecula, then he would be released. The next time he saw Thornton, Rea would be sitting on the witness stand in a courtroom.

Rea felt as if a massive weight had been lifted from his shoulders. He had never imagined he would become entangled with what most people would consider the embodiment of pure evil, but he knew he was doing the right thing by coming forward. He regretted that the memories of what he'd heard—all those young girls preyed upon and tortured—would probably linger long after the evidence was given in court. But that night, even though he was returning to a jail cell, Rea would be far away from Thornton and, for the first time, he would sleep a little easier.

Riverside, California
July 2003

Rounding the corner on his retirement, Hudson had his
eye on spending quality time with a fishing pole and his
horse. He was dating an attractive, blond artist, and they
contemplated selling their respective homes and pooling
their money to buy the ranch of their dreams, something
with a barn and corrals.

Hudson had less than a year before he concluded some
forty years in law enforcement, and he wanted to wrap up
this case, one of the most disturbing of his career. Hudson had unearthed quite a few prior victims, revealing
how Thornton and Snyder operated. Through their earlier crimes, Deputy District Attorney Michael Rushton
could demonstrate to jurors how Thornton had trained
Snyder to pick up girls, like Jessie Peters, Danyelle Cummins, and Michelle Curran using the two-hundred-plus
questions they had written in the green notebook. By
questioning Maria Rivera, Danyelle, and Elizabeth Holt,
he could show how the girls had been stalked. They
were conditioned by Snyder, who first became friendly
and intimate by sleeping and bathing with the victims,
then intimidated them with a firearms "lesson" in the desert.
The girls were drugged into submission, intimidated, and
conditioned. But these young victims who had been silenced in captivity could speak very clearly to the jury,
together, with one very powerful voice. The defendants'
pattern of conduct, as shown through testimony from
multiple victims, was admissible during the guilt phase of
the trial.

Learning that Jason Rea really had the goods on
Thornton was an unexpected retirement gift for Hudson.
Unable to wait to speak with his own defense attorney,
Rea had contacted a jail deputy at the jail, at great personal risk to himself, who questioned Rea briefly and
determined it was worthwhile for Hudson to speak with
him. Hudson was curious when Rea handed over Thorn-

ton's fifty-seven-page document, hoping it wasn't a Ted Kazyinski–inspired manifesto. Preliminary handwriting analysis showed that it was written by Thornton's hand. Together, Thornton's fifty-seven-page handwritten confession, and Rea's testimony on how he assembled it could nail the coffin shut on Thornton and Snyder and convince jurors to put them away forever.

In Riverside County, sheriff's department forensic technicians collected evidence. The DA's office decides what it wants to be examined, and the salient items of evidence are sent to the state crime lab, which had a facility in Riverside, for analysis. Unlike their fictional counterparts on television dramas, forensic experts don't carry guns and chase suspects, and cops don't have PhDs in biology, serology, toxicology, or microscopy, nor do they understand lab procedure for DNA analysis. By summertime, the state crime lab reports were crossing his desk, and Hudson reviewed the results and checked what needed analyzing before trial.

One half of the green spaghetti-strap top found in the hay outside the tack room did indeed match the other half found in the Suburban. The exertion of force against the shirt had produced the ripping of the fibers, suggesting it had been torn.

Preliminary forensic examinations showed that when Thornton and Snyder had hosed themselves and the body of Michelle Curran, they had effectively erased important blood and bodily fluids. Multiple examinations of the clothing worn by the defendants the day they were arrested failed to produce enough biological material for meaningful tests.

The most revealing forensics test was the gunshot residue test of Snyder's hands, which showed that she had indeed been the shooter. While this was a substantial result, additional concrete evidence was needed to seal their guilt.

The ballistics report on the Sylvia Springer shooting troubled Hudson, though it was not unexpected. The firearms examiner was unable to make a comparison because the only bullet recovered from the shooting had passed through Springer's shoulder and struck the ground, damaging the slug and rendering it unsuitable for comparison. The evidence they had linking Thornton and Snyder to the attack on Springer was circumstantial. They had money and a GMC motor home being transferred from Ricky J. Cartwright to Thornton; Pamela Bivens's testimony that she overheard the couple discussing the shooting, friends and drug buddies to whom Thornton and Snyder had bragged about being hit men, and a description from Springer's daughter. But Hudson couldn't conclusively put Thornton and Snyder at the scene. Nothing put a gun in Thornton's hands.

Hudson studied the Springer report, reviewed his notes, reread the original reports from the Tulsa PD, and looked at reports of the injuries Springer sustained in the attack, looking for anything he might have missed. And he got an idea.

Hudson excitedly dug through the report looking for phone numbers and called Sylvia Springer, who had moved with her children to another state to get far away from her former mother-in-law, Ricky J. Cartwright.

"This might be an off-the-wall kind of question," Hudson said, "but are those two bullets still in your body?"

"One is still in my neck next to the spine," Springer said. "The other is next to an artery, which is why the doctors left them in. Why do you ask?"

"Well," Hudson said, "do you know what condition those bullets are in?"

Springer said that both bullets were intact and the bullet in the thigh looked perfectly shaped in the X-ray.

After a few more phone calls, Hudson arranged a flight to the Midwest to see Springer and retrieve some evidence.

Weeks later, Hudson met Springer at a hospital, and while nurses prepped her for the procedure, surgical assistants helped Hudson scrub in; he donned sterile gloves, a head covering, and a mask. He entered the operating room and watched the surgeon make a small cut in Springer's thigh. Over the years the bullet had worked itself away from the femoral artery in the leg and closer to the surface of the skin, making its removal a simple task that posed scant risk.

Hudson watched the surgery, thinking to himself that he had never witnessed the retrieval of a bullet from the victim of a crime who was still alive. He was happy that Springer had agreed to the minor surgery. She had been carrying around a bit of evidence inside of her, and if there was a chance that it could conclusively link Thornton to the attack, she was glad to comply. When the doctor removed the bullet, Hudson was ready with an evidence container, also sterilized. He thanked the doctor and, in order to preserve the chain of custody for evidence, he immediately labeled it and boarded a plane back to Riverside, where he submitted it to the sheriff's crime lab for a ballistics examination.

Before long, the firearms examiner had results. The bullet removed from Springer shared significant and distinctive markings suggesting that it was most likely fired from the .38 Taurus that had been found in the pocket of Thornton's wet Levi's in the Motel 6 room. In layperson's terms, it was a match.

By the time Hudson retired the next year, the case was set for trial. He felt that he had done as much as he could and hoped for the best result. Finally closing the chapter of his life marked by years of witnessing murder, misery, and heartbreak, Hudson felt assured that this last grisly case would reach a satisfying conclusion at the hands of the legal system. Like a hero from an old western, Hudson remarried in retirement and started a new life on his ranch, happily riding off into the sunset with his new bride.

Epilogue

Before ordinary citizens show up at the courthouse to report for jury duty, they are warned that they will be bored. Even official juror information pamphlets advise jurors to supply themselves with reading material, needlework, or a laptop computer, or be content with watching daytime television while waiting to be called. With this ominous preview of the judicial system, potential jurors arrive at the courthouse armed with tote bags stuffed with magazines and crossword puzzles. Prospective jurors are herded into courtrooms, scrutinized by attorneys, and spend days waiting, despite the recent jury system reforms designed to reduce downtime. By the time they get assigned to a trial, jurors arrive on the first day of testimony expecting more of the same. The system doesn't disappoint.

Any prosecutor would be overjoyed to transport jurors to the crime scene in a time machine so that they can witness the crime occurring, see the fright on the victim's face the instant the trigger is pulled. Observing the accused at the time the offense is committed is far different from seeing them after they have lived behind bars for several years and are softened by a diet of fatty jail food, sporting clean-cut, suburban hair styles, and wearing clothes that a defense attorney believes will make a good impression with the average juror. Legendary defense attorney Leslie Abramson, who represented brothers Lyle and Erik Menendez for the shotgun murders of their parents, dressed her clients in pastel sweaters and dress slacks. The wealthy brothers' attire made them resemble gentlemen of privilege fresh off the tennis court of their estate, not selfish sons who slaughtered their parents to hasten the disbursement of their inheritance.

Thus, the sanitized versions of Michael Forrest Thornton and Janeen Marie Snyder appeared before the Honorable Judge Paul E. Zellerbach in Department 44 of Riverside Superior Court and before the panel of prospective jurors that spilled into the courtroom gallery. Gone were the physiques made lean by a constant diet of methamphetamine and the occasional meal. Gone were the ripped jeans, black boots, and sullen glares. Snyder's once bleached blond hair had grown out to its natural mousy brown. Snyder's attorneys, Michael Belter and Chris Harmon, dressed her in a business casual wardrobe of colorful jackets and skirts, clothes the mothers of her victims might wear. Representing Thornton, veteran defense attorneys Peter Scalisi and David Macher took advantage of their client's age. Their forty-nine-year-old client was no longer the man who once fancied himself a modern-day Charles Manson, lording over a pack of beautiful young girls and an empire of sex, drugs, and violence. The newly transformed Thornton was an unassuming, harmless-looking middle-aged fellow who looked as though he had been dispatched to repair the office photocopy machine. His graying, thinning hair had been trimmed by the jail barber into a modified flat-top. He was costumed in short-sleeved, white shirts, unfashionable ties, and too-tight dark slacks that made him look more vaguely uncomfortable than dangerous. The makeover made Thornton nearly unrecognizable to his former drug buddies.

The state of California sought to convict both defendants of capital murder for killing Michelle Curran, and to execute them both. They faced additional charges of kidnapping, burglary, and sexual assault with a foreign object. Thornton and Snyder also faced four special allegations, charging that the murder had been committed during the course of a kidnapping, burglary, sexual assault, and during the infliction of torture. If the jury convicted either of the defendants of murder and found any one of the special circumstances to be true, it would trigger the second phase of the trial, known as the penalty phase. In the next phase, jurors would hear additional evidence in order to decide whether to recommend the death penalty or life in prison without possibility of parole for the convicted defendant.

A capital defendant is entitled to a team of two defense attorneys who are provided a generous expense account, supervised by the judge, for investigators and other expenses required to defend their client. The defendants' clothing and shoes for trial are purchased from this account. If the state has sought the death penalty against capital defendants, the reasoning is that they should be dressed well during their trial.

Capital murder trials carry such high stakes that trials stagger at a glacial cadence under the weight of legal maneuvering. While they have their moments, these trials usually lack the dramatic gravitas and immediacy portrayed in television courtroom dramas. Protocol discourages vanity outbursts by lawyers or spectators, and reciprocal evidence-sharing rules prevent surprise witnesses or pulling a bloody knife from thin air. Forensic technicians at real crime scenes make no instant proclamations regarding the time or cause of death, and rarely do they unearth one perfect, finger-pointing piece of evidence that conclusively proves a defendant's guilt, if there ever was such a thing.

The story of Thornton and Snyder, and of their many victims, began with Rushton's opening statement. His challenge was to chisel away at the fresh-scrubbed veneer of these defendants in the emotionally stale courtroom and reveal the true nature of their conduct through the testimony of the witnesses who had experienced the horror and escaped. He could shape the arc and pace of the trial by the sequence in which he presented the witnesses and the way their testimony unfolded. He had to decide which of the hundreds of crime scene photos clearly depicted the elements of each criminal count, while battling the defense attorneys' attempts to keep jurors from seeing them at all.

Rushton had hundreds of crime-scene photos from which to choose. The first officers to arrive took photos, as did the forensic technicians. The ranch was examined and reexamined again and again. Whether jurors would ever see the photos or the other evidence that had been painstakingly collected by police and technicians was the source of fierce conflicts between the lawyers. This was not uncommon: many a case would be won or lost via pretrial dustups before a single juror entered the courtroom. Judge Zellerbach refereed the arguments by counsel, then ruled. For more than a year prior to jury selection, the legal skirmishes scorched hundreds of pages of legal motions as the defense and the prosecution staked legal claims to the evidence and sought to establish the procedural footprint that would best suit them for the trial. In Thornton's case, the judge's rulings shaped the content and structure of the trial that allowed the lawyers to craft trial strategy.

The major procedural issue presented to Judge Zellerbach was whether to have one trial for both defendants or to split the case and hold separate trials. The defense argued vigorously for holding separate trials, which meant that each witness would testify in court twice, once for

each trial. Judge Zellerbach denied that motion as well as
the defense attorneys' subsequent legal requests to hold
only one trial with a separate jury for each defendant.
However, he did grant the defense attorneys' final request
to split the penalty phase of the trial. The final configura-
tion would be to hold one trial for both defendants, in
which one jury would decide the guilt of both defendants.
If they found the defendants guilty, the same jury first
would be presented with testimony and evidence regarding Snyder, in order to decide whether to punish her with
the death penalty or life in prison without possibility of
parole. After deliberating and deciding her fate, the same
jury would begin the second penalty phase with evidence
and testimony related to Thornton. Once the jury had decided the fate of both defendants, Judge Zellerbach would
make the final decision regarding their punishment.

The defense filed additional motions which, if revealed
to jurors, might either have brightened their boring day in
court or dimmed their view of the justice system. The defense asked the judge to rule the death penalty unconstitu-
tional and contrary to the International Covenant on
International Rights, a jurisdictional stretch for a state
court judge, and then asked him to forestall imposition of
the death penalty under the theory that it was a cruel and
unusual punishment prohibited by the Eighth Amend-
ment of the Constitution. They also asked that Michelle
Curran not be referred to as a "victim," finding that term
prejudicial to their clients. All of these motions were denied.

The judge's rulings in these motions triggered additional strategic decisions on the part of the defense. Snyder's defense team assumed the risky strategy of pitting
their client against Thornton, painting her as another victim of his manipulation, who was influenced at an early
age and had no safe haven to escape his influence. The
strategy was risky because the jurors would eventually
hear that it was Snyder who shot Michelle. Thornton's
defense team took their own gamble by suggesting that

Thornton, Snyder, and their young victim had been engaged in a voluntary sex game in the tack room that had turned deadly by mistake and killed Michelle Curran.

If it had been up to the defense, the prosecution's evidence and witness list would have been gutted and jurors would have seen very little of the evidence and testimony. Defense attorneys made dozens of requests to exclude certain items of evidence, including autopsy photographs, Michelle Curran's tiny jeans, shoes, and shirt, the stacks of ammunition and firearms that were not used in the murder, and the audio tapes that Thornton had made while he, Snyder, and Michelle Curran were in their motel room, and while the three cruised around Rubidoux looking for eight-year-old Brittany Perkins at her school bus stop just hours before the murder in the tack room.

Rushton sought to introduce the defendants' interactions with victims Jessie Peters, Sylvia Springer, Maria Rivera, Danyelle Cummins, Brittany Perkins, Elizabeth Holt, and Rene Pardo. The introduction of this testimony bolstered evidence of the defendants' pattern of conduct, motive, and intent. The issue was complicated by the contrary defense positions, which pitted the lawyers against one another in a three-way battle. Attorneys Scalisi and Macher fought bitterly to exclude evidence or testimony from these additional witnesses, but Snyder's attorneys found that this evidence helped with her defense because Thornton, they alleged, had used the same manipulative tactics on her. Just as he had used intimidation, sexual assault, and drugs to manipulate the other victims, he had used them to condition Snyder. It was similar to illegal get-rich-quick schemes where a con men hooks innocent investors, who then convince their own friends and family to join the scheme. In the same way, Snyder's attorneys sought to argue, Thornton had tricked Snyder into becoming a perpetrator. Thornton set upon shaping Snyder at such a young age and became her role model in luring the other victims. The testimony from other victims would prove that Snyder was acting in the way Thornton had programmed her, Snyder's defense argued, and had been subjected to similar treatment when she was the age of the victims.

David Macher, Thornton's defense attorney, argued vehemently against allowing the evidence of Jessie Peters's murder because the body had never been recovered and, thus, there was no proof she had been murdered. The bulk of the evidence came from Thornton's ex-wife, an unreliable witness, according to Macher, because she harbored ill will toward her husband, and the admission of this evidence would amount to an unfair trial-within-a-trial. Macher also argued against allowing testimony from Maria Rivera, who he claimed had fabricated the whole episode at the house on Silver Circle. Airing this evidence amounted to a dangerous digression, far from the question at hand: whether or not Thornton killed Michelle Curran.

Rushton said that the evidence of the prior victims fell well within the bounds of the law that allows the prosecution to show similar pattern of conduct, even if those acts are uncharged offenses. If Thornton's attorneys planned to concoct a tale that Michelle Curran *wanted* to be bound with duct tape, *wanted* multiple zip ties around her wrists, and *wanted* to be gagged, bound, and hung from ropes in a barn while being sexually assaulted, jurors needed to hear from this couple's prior victims who suffered sexual assault via force and fear. Ultimately, Judge Zellerbach admitted the evidence of the other victims to demonstrate the defendants' pattern of conduct and their "common plan or scheme." He also admitted evidence generated by the defendants. The audio recordings and the Polaroid photographs Thornton took of Michelle Curran while she was their captive were arguably the most damning evidence against them. Judge Zellerbach admitted these recordings and the Polaroids, too.

With this evidence, Rushton now faced a very different set of challenges. In outlining his trial strategy, his opening statement, the sequence of witnesses, and the content of their testimony, Rushton had juggled several priorities.

As a prosecutor representing the state of California, he bore the burden of proof. He had to present enough evidence and testimony to convince all twelve jurors that both defendants were guilty of each element of each offense. The defense, on the other hand, needed to plant the seeds of doubt in only one juror out of the twelve. A sole juror who voted for the defense in an 11–1 verdict, for example, would trigger a mistrial unless the judge ordered the jury to resume deliberations, during which time the dissenting juror could convince others to jump ship and vote for the defense. Rushton had to present a case so foolproof and legally airtight that all twelve jurors would believe unanimously that the defendants were guilty beyond a reasonable doubt.

Finally, after all the haggling, the attorneys attended to some legal housekeeping before jury selection and the official start of trial. But even as the first batch of jurors were told to put away their books, magazines, and electronic devices and report to Department 44, there was still something missing.

Of the hundreds of photographs and thousands of pages of police interviews with nearly one hundred witnesses, there was only one truly unique item of evidence—Thornton's fifty-seven-page jailhouse manifesto. In his own handwriting, Thornton had described in detail how, when, and why he and Snyder had snatched Michelle Curran off the street in Las Vegas and traveled for two weeks back and forth to California in a nightmarish journey that ended in a bloodbath in the tack room of a Riverside horse ranch. Jason Rea's testimony would put the lie to Thornton's defense posture that he, Snyder, and their victim were engaged in consensual sexual activity and that Michelle Curran was anything other than a helpless victim. As Thornton's hand-picked confidant, Rea could testify about Thornton's twisted plan to manipulate Michelle Curran in the same way he and Snyder had manipulated their other victims and reveal his intentions to stage-manage their trial.

And therein lay the problem: Rea had been transported to the district attorney's office on March 27, 2003, where he signed an agreement stating that he would testify in the case and promised to return to court in July 2003 for sentencing on his drug possession and bad checks cases. Rea signed the agreement and walked out of the DA's office.

Then he disappeared.

With prospective jurors filing into the courtroom, the stage was set and the trial started without, arguably, one of the prosecution's most important witnesses.

**Riverside Superior Court
January 10, 2006**

"This is Michelle Curran." Deputy District Attorney Michael Rushton held a photo of the attractive, smiling teenager for jurors.

"In April of 2001, Michelle Curran was a sixteen-year-old girl living with her family in Las Vegas, Nevada, attending Western High School," Rushton said. "She had a tight group of friends, like sixteen-year-old people do. Their friends can be their lives, and in this case, that was Michelle."

With this introduction, Rushton skillfully drew jurors into the world of a young woman on the cusp of adulthood, balancing her obsession with fashion, her infatuation with her first serious boyfriend, her friends, her first real job, and her schoolwork. After Rushton's remarks, jurors heard the opening statements from both defense attorneys outlining their opposing views of the case. The first witness to testify was Michelle's sister, Tiffani, followed by other family members, her friends, and her boyfriend, Steve, who talked about Michelle's life and their bewilderment at her disappearance. Michelle's heartbroken grandmother died not long after her abduction. Each witness testified that even though Michelle got up in the morning and went to bed at night with a cell phone attached to one ear, no one heard from her after she had vanished. Ranch owner Diane Lindholm spoke of coming home to hear the gunshot, residents of the Loring Ranch development described watching the couple hopping fences, and police officers dispatched to the neighborhood described the frantic search before Thornton was apprehended in a side yard and Snyder was pulled out from underneath a desk at Rancho Jurupa Park. Officers of every stripe described the serial searches of the Loring Ranch neighborhood, the Lindholm ranch, and Rancho Jurupa Park. Detectives and forensic technicians gave details of the extensive searches of the Suburban, the Motel 6 room in Rubidoux, the former family home on Silver Circle, Thornton's mother's house in Mesa, Arizona, the Running Springs cabin, and the home in Lake Arrowhead and repeated searches of the ranch, the park, and the Loring Ranch neighborhood in search of the murder weapon and the body of a victim. Police detectives testified about recovering Michelle's body from the horse trailer and the additional searches of the ranch. Forensic technicians gave jurors a brief tutorial about processing a crime scene and collecting evidence as they introduced each item of evidence. Rushton traced Michelle's usual route to school and Thornton and Snyder's stay at the Las Vegas Best Western. Motel clerks and bellhops identified motel receipts and photos of the defendants and victim on their sojourn from Las Vegas to Lake Arrowhead, Arizona, and back to Riverside.

Rushton methodically walked jurors through Michelle's final days with testimony from meth-addled friends of Thornton and Snyder, who were dealers and visitors to the former Thornton family house on Silver Circle. During a break in the trial, several witnesses who were still addicted to meth demonstrated clear symptoms of withdrawal in the back of the courtroom. Jurors heard about the disappearance and murder of Jessie Peters from Pamela Bivens, the salon employees, and the grieving mother,

Cheryle Peters. They heard horrific accounts of sexual assault and violence from Maria Rivera, Elizabeth Holt, Brittany Perkins, and Sylvia Springer. Danyelle Cummins and her mother testified that the details handwritten by Thornton and Snyder in the green spiral-bound journal were all true, and that they had moved shortly after those observations had been recorded in the journal.

Scientific technicians who examined hair and fibers, ballistics, tool marks, and shoe and tire impressions testified that the items of evidence found at the ranch matched evidence found in the Suburban or in the hotel room. The tire impressions matched the tires on the Suburban. The boot mark on Lindholm's window matched the sole of Snyder's boot. The bullet recovered from Michelle Curran matched Snyder's gun. No fingerprints were found in the tack room, from the windows or frames of Lindholm's ranch, or in the trailer. The blood on the walls of the tack room belonged to Michelle Curran. Hosing down her remains in the tack room effectively removed biological evidence of her attackers, but gunshot residue taken from Snyder's hands showed that she had recently fired a gun. The duct tape found on Michelle Curran's wrists matched rolls of duct tape found in the Suburban. The coroner testified about the marks on the victim's body that led them to conclude that wounds in her genital area were caused by sexual assault with a foreign object. Bank officials testified about the transfer of funds from accounts belonging to Ricky J. Cartwright and Michael Thornton.

Rene Pardo testified about flirting online with Pamela Bivens and their hours-long fling at a Los Angeles motel, which was followed by a prolonged and frightening series of threats via computer by Michael Thornton. Pardo told jurors that as the president and creator of a Canadian firm on the frontlines of software and computer technology, he had been astonished by Thornton's knowledge and technical expertise and the speed with which had tracked him online.

Riverside Superior Court
March 9, 2006

Rushton had arrived at the end of his witness list. He was close to resting the prosecution phase of the case, after which point the defense would present just a few witnesses apiece. The lawyers were preparing to review more than nine hundred items of evidence that had been marked as exhibits during the trial, and he was slogging through testimony from Henry Ong, a forensic computer analyst with master's degrees in math, computer science, and physics. A lieutenant commander in the navy for thirteen years, Ong had been a military computer specialist but was currently conducting forensic computer analysis for the DA's office. Ong testified that his examination of Thornton's home and laptop computers showed that Thornton "knew more than I back in those years, 2000, 2001." Some of the files that Thornton had hidden on his computer carried levels of encryption so complex that according to Ong's testimony, it would take a computer one hundred years to decipher the code. This demonstrated a surprising level of sophistication for 2001 that most people, even years later, would never possess.

Before continuing with Ong's testimony, defense attorney Belter addressed the court.

"Your honor, something has come to our attention," Belter said. "There's a witness we've been trying to locate for some time. His name is Jason Rea, R-e-a. We were unable to locate him, but he has apparently picked up a new case. He's in the building today."

After lying low for three years, Rea had been picked up on a minor traffic violation a few days earlier and was currently in custody. Rushton and Belter, both of whom considered Rea a valuable witness, nearly fell over themselves trying to convince Judge Zellerbach to make certain that Rea was not released from custody, at least until they'd had a chance to speak with him about testifying. Up until this point, Rushton had not introduced to jurors the handwritten fifty-seven-page document that Thornton had produced behind bars because Rea had "fallen off the face of the earth," in Rushton's words.

Unfortunately, much of the drama that a live courtroom does produce is never witnessed by jurors. When Rea arrived in the courtroom—the reluctant accomplice who had become the reluctant witness—no jurors were present. Rea took one look at Thornton and knew that he was still using drugs, even behind bars. While Rea was locked up with him, Thornton had snorted Wellbutrin, a prescription drug typically taken orally, but it acts like methamphetamine when snorted. From his seat at the defense table, Thornton greeted Rea with a small wave by wiggling a few fingers. Rea kept his usual straight face and didn't react, but he thought that Thornton had to be smarter than that. Doesn't he have any idea Rea wondered, that I'm here to testify for the *prosecution?* Did Thornton really believe that Rea was his puppet and would dutifully repeat what he had told him?

Rea had been reluctant to testify, but fear was not his primary concern. He had thought long and hard about cooperating with the prosecution once he learned that Rushton was seeking the death penalty. A former altar boy, Rea had been raised Catholic and did not believe in the death penalty. Even though Thornton and Snyder had killed, he did not believe that more bloodshed was the solution.

Getting to know Thornton had turned Rea's life upside down, making him question his religion, his life, and everything he believed. After he was released from custody, Rea had struggled mightily with his months confined with a monster behind bars, wondering why Thornton had chosen him, of all people, to share his most disturbing secrets. Rea went to church and prayed, exploring what was wrong with him. He could not erase Thornton from his mind and was haunted by the sick glow on Thornton's face when he had described the moment when he and Snyder ended Michelle Curran's life. For months, Rea had suppressed his revulsion at the details Thornton had spewed, reenacting the way he had bound and gagged Michelle in the tack room. Thornton became so engrossed in recreating the tack room scene that he bore a look of ecstasy, particularly when he came to the part of the story when Michelle, gagged and unable to talk, realized that she was not going to be untied. Thornton told Rea that he "loved the look on her face when she realized that she wasn't going to get away and that she was going to die."

Thornton had had the tack room scenario planned far ahead on several levels. The same sophistication Thornton used harnessing computer technology also went into planning what to do if he and Snyder were ever caught. Like the script he and Snyder created to approach young girls, he wrote up a script for Snyder about men chasing her after their flight from the Lindholm ranch. But the events of the days and the night prior to Michelle's murder were also part of Thornton's plan.

Thornton and Snyder were extremely secure in their relationship. What perplexed Rea was the suggestion that Thornton wanted to "replace" Snyder with Michelle, or that Snyder was getting jealous of the younger girl. But Snyder had nothing to worry about. Thornton never planned on replacing her with Michelle. It was part of Thornton's multi-level strategy. He always had everything planned out—*everything*. Michelle was chosen to be Snyder's first kill, so Snyder would fire her own gun, with her bullet and gunshot residue on her hands. If something went awry and they were arrested, Thornton wanted a safe haven for himself. He thought like a prosecutor: what motive would a middle-aged man have to shoot a beautiful young girl who would have sex with him? But Snyder? One could argue that Snyder was jealous, or that she was afraid of being replaced by a younger, prettier girl. A few days before the murder, Thornton had provoked a few arguments with Snyder in full view of their friends, one at a restaurant and another at a friend's house where the three had stayed over the weekend. He paid special attention to Michelle, which he knew would irritate Snyder. Since he had programmed Snyder from the time she was fourteen, he knew how to push her buttons. Snyder took the bait and unwittingly acted the part of the jealous girlfriend. He picked another fight with Snyder, again in front of their friends, the night before Michelle was killed. The next day, Thornton planned to give Snyder the order to shoot Michelle when he wanted her to.

Thornton took sick pleasure in manipulating Michelle, who was bound by physical restraints, and Snyder, his other victim, who was enmeshed in psychological shackles. Snyder, the wounded, jealous girlfriend, would shoot and kill the innocent victim with her own gun. If they didn't get caught, they would both be off the hook. If something went wrong, Thornton had his exit strategy, his safety deposit box. And the prosecution had swallowed it, hook, line and sinker.

The strategic labyrinth, including Thornton's attempts to manipulate Rea behind bars, angered Rea because Thornton had never assumed responsibility for any of his actions. Thornton blamed his father for molesting him as a child, which he said had ushered him toward a criminal lifestyle, but Rea thought that was ludicrous. Thornton had everything he ever wanted—a million-dollar business, a chain of stores, a wife, a family. He was the one who had tossed it all away. Rea had been molested as a boy by the parish priest and was offended that Thornton had used it as an excuse instead of taking responsibility for his actions.

Rea eventually came to the conclusion that he was not responsible for making the decision to recommend the death penalty. Each juror carried that responsibility. The issue boiled down to the fact that Rea knew that Thornton had committed these crimes. He knew in his heart that Thornton was guilty.

Having made that decision, Rea cooperated with the prosecution and testified against Thornton. As the words flowed from the witness stand, Rea saw the rage in a slow crawl across Thornton's face. He felt cleansed—and a little scared—but he put the fear out of his mind and was grateful that the deputies in the courtroom were armed.

After hearing all of the evidence from both the prosecution and the defense, jurors unanimously found Thornton and Snyder guilty of all charges. In separate death penalty phases, they recommended capital punishment for both defendants.

Janeen Marie Snyder is currently in the California Institute for Women in Chowchilla, California, awaiting a sentence of death. Michael Forrest Thornton is confined to death row at San Quentin Prison in California. Under California law, all capital cases are automatically subject to appellate review. The standard waiting period between sentencing and execution is twenty-five years.